NYSTCE 116

English to Speakers of Other Languages (ESOL)

Teacher Certification Exam

Sharon A Wynne, M.S.

XAMonline, INC.

Boston

To obtain permission(s) to use the material from this work for any purpose including workshops or seminars, please submit a written request to:

XAMonline, Inc.
21 Orient Avenue
Melrose, MA 02176
Toll Free 1-800-509-4128
Email: info@xamonline.com
Web www.xamonline.com
Fax: 1-617-583-5552

Library of Congress Cataloging-in-Publication Data

Wynne, Sharon A.
NYSTCE English to Speakers of Other Languages (ESOL) 116: Teacher Certification/ Sharon A. Wynne. ISBN 978-1-60787- 478-2

1. English to Speakers of Other Languages (ESOL)   2. Study Guides.
3. NYSTCE   4. Teachers' Certification & Licensure.   5. Careers

Disclaimer:
The opinions expressed in this publication are the sole works of XAMonline and were created independently from the National Education Association, Educational Testing Service, and any State Department of Education, National Evaluation Systems or other testing affiliates.

Between the time of publication and printing, state-specific standards as well as testing formats and website information may make changes that are not included in part or whole within this product. Sample test questions are developed by XAMonline and reflect content similar to real tests; however, they are not former tests. XAMonline assembles content that aligns with state standards but makes no claims nor guarantees teacher candidates a passing score. Numerical scores are determined by testing companies such as NES or ETS and are compared with individual state standards. A passing score varies from state to state.

Printed in the United States of America

NYSTCE English to Speakers of Other Languages (ESOL) 116
ISBN 978-1-60787-478-2

About XAMonline

Founded in 1996, XAMonline began with one teacher in training who was frustrated by the lack of materials available for certification exam preparation. From a single state-specific guide, XAMonline has grown to offer guides for every state exam, as well as the PRAXIS series.

Each study guide offers more than just the competencies and skills required to pass the test. The core text material leads the teacher beyond rote memorization of skills to mastery of subject matter, a necessary step for effective teaching. XAMonline's unique publishing model brings currency and innovation to teacher preparation.

- Print-on-demand technology allows for the most up-to-date guides that are first to market when tests change or are updated.
- The highest quality standards are maintained by using seasoned, professional teachers who are experts in their fields to author the guides.
- Each guide includes varied levels of rigor in a comprehensive practice test so that the study experience closely matches the actual in-test experience.
- The content of the guides is relevant and engaging.

At its inception, XAMonline was a forward-thinking company, and we remain committed to bring new ways of studying and learning to the teaching profession. We choose from a pool of over 1500 certified teachers to review, edit, and write our guides. We partner with technology firms to bring innovation to study habits, offering online test functionality, a personalized flash card builder, and ebooks that allow teachers in training to make personal notes, highlight, and study the material in a variety of ways.

To date, XAMonline has helped nearly 500,000 teachers pass their certification or licensing exam. Our commitment to preparation exceeds the expectation of simply providing the proper material for study; it extends from helping teachers gain mastery of the subject matter and giving them the tools to become the most effective classroom leaders possible to ushering today's students towards a successful future.

TEACHER CERTIFICATION STUDY GUIDE

TABLE OF CONTENTS

How to Use This Book

Help! Where do I begin?

Begin at the beginning. Our informal polls show that most people begin studying up to 8 weeks prior to the test date, so start early. Then ask yourself some questions: How much do you really know? Are you coming to the test straight from your teacher education program or are you reviewing subjects you haven't considered in 10 years? Either way, take a diagnostic or assessment test first. Also, spend time on sample tests so that you become accustomed to the way the actual test will appear.

A diagnostic can help you decide how to manage your study time and reveal things about your compendium of knowledge. Although this guide is structured to follow the order of the test, you are not required to study in that order. By finding a time-management and study plan that fits your life, you will be more effective. The results of your diagnostic or self-assessment test can be a guide for how to manage your time and point you towards areas that needs more attention.

You may also want to structure your study time based on the percentage of questions on the test. For example, 25% of the mathematics questions focus on algebraic concepts. **Note:** this doesn't mean that algebra is equal to a 25% of the test's worth. Remember the distribution charts: each major content area is devoted an equal amount of questions, but within the content areas the number of questions per subject area varies greatly. Depending on your grasp of any one topic, you may want to devote time comparable to the number of questions. See the example study rubric below for an idea of how you might structure your study plan.

Week	Activity
8 weeks prior to test	Take a diagnostic or pre-assessment test, then build your study plan accordingly to your time availability and areas that need the most work.
7 weeks prior to test	Read the entire study guide. This does not have to be an in-depth reading, but you should take the time to mark sections or areas you know you'd like to return to or that can be skimmed in further study.
6-3 weeks prior to test	For each of these 4 weeks, choose a content area to study. You don't have to go in the order of the book. It may be that you start with the content that needs the most review. Alternatively, you may want to ease yourself into your plan by starting with the most familiar material.
2 weeks prior to test	Take the sample test, score it, and create a review plan for the final week before the test.
1 week prior to test	Following your plan (which will likely be aligned with the areas that need the most review), go back and study the sections that align with the questions you missed. Then go back and study the sections related to the questions you answered correctly. If need be, create flashcards and drill yourself on any area that you makes you anxious.

About the NYSTCE Field 116: English to Speakers of Other Language Exam

The exam seeks to ensure that all ESOL teachers working in New York State understand and are ready to implement research- and evidence-based teaching and assessment practices to ensure that English Language Learners (ELLs) develop both language proficiency and content-area knowledge.

There are two sections to the exam. The first consists of selected-response questions while the other is a constructed-response. The constructed-response portion of the test incorporates one or more 'artifacts' that a teacher of English for Speakers of Other Languages (ESOL) would likely encounter (student work samples, commonly used assessment tools, etc.) in his/her educational role. The test creates a scenario that requires you to analyze the artifacts supplied. This guide contains examples of the type of artifacts you may encounter; the NYSTCE website also includes samples. Together, the two sections are designed to measure a teacher's content-area knowledge as well as his/her knowledge of evidence-based and research-supported teaching methods.

Total testing time is 195 minutes. According to the test designers, the selected-response portion of the test should take up to 135 minutes while the constructed-response time is expected to take up to 60 minutes. This is a computer-based exam. The computer will monitor both the amount of time you have remaining and allow you to easily navigate to questions that you have not yet completed.

The selected-response section of the test counts for 80% of your final score and the constructed-response counts for the remaining 20%. Within the selected-response section, all questions have the same value in calculating your final score. Below you can find a breakdown of the overall scoring of the exam both by competency and overall section.

Test Format	Computer-Based Test (CBT)
Total Time	195 minutes
Question Format	90 Selected Response questions 1 Constructed response
Question Weight	Selected Response- 80% Constructed response 20 %

Selected-response

Competency 1 - Language and Language Learning
This section consists of approximately 15 questions and is worth approximately 13% of your total score.

Competency 2 - Knowledge of English Language Learners
This section consists of approximately 15 questions and is worth approximately 13% of your total score.

Competency 3 - ESOL Instructional Planning, Practices, and Assessment
This section consists of approximately 15 questions and is worth approximately 13% of your total score.

Competency 4 - Instructing English Language Learners in English Language Arts
This section consists of approximately 15 questions and is worth approximately 14% of your total score.

Competency 5 - Instructing English Language Learners in the Content Areas
This section consists of approximately 15 questions and is worth approximately 14% of your total score.

Competency 6 - ESOL Professional Environments
This section consists of approximately 15 questions and is worth approximately 13% of your total score.

Constructed Response

Competency 7 - Analysis, Synthesis, and Application
This section consists of one scenario requiring you to analyze common artifacts (such as work samples) and is worth 20% of your total score.

Other Helpful Study and Testing Tips

What you study is as important as **how** you study. You can increase your chances of mastering the information by taking some simple, effective steps.

<u>Study Tips</u>

1. You are what you eat. Good eating habits while studying and on the day of the test are very important. Eating well and staying hydrated help you learn and retain information. In addition, certain foods contain compounds that help increase neurotransmitter levels, supporting memory and recall of information. Eating the following foods will support your hungry brain as you study and learn.

- Milk
- Nuts and seeds
- Rice
- Whole grains
- Eggs

- Turkey
- Vegetables
- Fish

The better you eat, the better you'll feel as you study and, most importantly, on the day of the exam!

1. The pen is mightier than the sword. Learn to take great notes. A by-product of our modern culture is that we have grown accustomed to getting our information in short doses. We've subconsciously trained ourselves to assimilate information into neat little packages. Messy notes fragment the flow of information. Your notes can be much clearer with proper formatting. The Cornell Method is one such format. This method was popularized in *How to Study in College,* Ninth Edition, by Walter Pauk. You can benefit from the method without purchasing an additional book by simply looking the method up online. On the next page is a sample of how *The Cornell Method* can be adapted for use with this guide.

← 2 ½" →	← 6" →
Cue Column	**Note-Taking Column** 1. **Record:** During your reading, use the note-taking column to record important points. 2. **Questions:** As soon as you finish a section, formulate questions based on the notes in the right-hand column. Writing questions helps to clarify meanings, reveal relationships, establish community, and strengthen memory. Also, the writing of questions sets the stage for exam study later. 3. **Recite:** Cover the note-taking column with a sheet of paper. Then, looking at the questions or cue words in the question and cue column only, say aloud, in your own words, the answers to the questions, facts, or ideas indicated by the cue words. 4. **Reflect:** Reflect on the material by asking yourself questions. 5. **Review:** Spend at least ten minutes every week reviewing all your previous notes. Doing so helps you retain ideas and topics for the exam.
↑ Summary 2" ↓	After reading, use this space to summarize the notes from each page.

*Adapted from *How to Study in College,* Ninth Edition, by Walter Pauk, ©2008 Wadsworth

2. See the forest and the trees. In other words, get the concept before you look at the details. One way to do this is to take notes as you read, paraphrasing or summarizing in your own words. Putting the concept in terms that are comfortable and familiar may increase retention.

3. Question authority. Ask why, why, why. Pull apart written material paragraph by paragraph and don't forget the captions under the illustrations. For example, if a heading reads *Stream Erosion* put it in the form of a question. (Why do streams erode? Or what is stream erosion?) Then find the answer within the material. If you train your mind to think in this manner you will learn more and prepare yourself for answering test questions.

4. Play mind games. Using your brain for reading or puzzles keeps it flexible. Even with a limited amount of time your brain can take in data (much like a computer) and store it for later use. In ten minutes you can: read two paragraphs (at least), quiz yourself with flash cards, or review notes. Even if you don't fully understand something on the first pass, your mind stores it for recall, which is why frequent reading or review increases chances of retention and comprehension.

5. Place yourself in exile and set the mood. . Set aside a particular place and time to study that best suits your personal needs. If you're a night person, burn the midnight oil. If you're a morning person set yourself up with some coffee and get to it. Make your study time and place as free from distraction as possible and surround yourself with what you need, be it silence or music. Studies have shown that music can aid in concentration, absorption, and retrieval of information. Not all music, though. Research indicates that classical music is most effective.

6. Get pointed in the right direction. Use arrows to point to important passages or pieces of information. It's easier to read than a page full of yellow highlights. Highlighting can be used sparingly, but add an arrow to the margin to call attention to it.

7. Check your time budget. You should at least review all the content material before your test, but allocate the most time to the areas that need the most refreshing. It sounds obvious, but it's easy to forget. You can use the study rubric above to balance your study budget.

> The proctor will write the start time where it can be seen and then, later, provide the time remaining, typically 15 minutes before the end of the test.

And Another Thing

Question Types

You're probably thinking, enough already, I want to study! Indulge us a little longer while we explain that there is actually more than one type of multiple-choice question. You can thank us later after you realize how well prepared you are for your exam.

1. **Complete the Statement.** The name says it all. In this question type you'll be asked to choose the correct completion of a given statement. For example: The list of Dolch Basic Sight Words is a relatively short list of words that children should be able to:

    a. Sound out
    b. Know the meaning of
    c. Recognize on sight
    d. Use in a sentence

    The correct answer is C. In order to check your answer, test out the statement by adding each of the choices to the end of it.

2. **Which of the Following.** One way to test your answer choice for this type of question is to replace the phrase "which of the following" with your selection. Use this example: Which of the following words is one of the twelve most frequently used in children's reading texts:

    a. There
    b. This
    c. The
    d. An

    Don't look! Test your answer. _____ is one of the twelve most frequently used in children's reading texts. Did you guess C? Then you guessed correctly.

3. **Roman Numeral Choices.** This question type is used when there is more than one possible correct answer. For example: Which of the following two arguments accurately supports the use of cooperative learning as an effective method of instruction?

    I.   Cooperative learning groups facilitate healthy competition between individuals in the group.

    II.   Cooperative learning groups allow academic achievers to carry or cover for academic underachievers.

    III.   Cooperative learning groups make each student in the group accountable for the success of the group.

    IV.   Cooperative learning groups make it possible for students to reward other group members for achieving.

        a. I and II
        b. II and III
        c. I and III
        d. III and IV

Notice that the question states there are **two** possible answers. It's best to read all the possibilities first before looking at the answer choices. In this case, the correct answer is D.

4. **Negative Questions.** This type of question contains words such as "not," "least," and "except." Each correct answer will be the statement that does **not** fit the situation described in the question. Such as: Multicultural education is **not**

        a. An idea or concept
        b. A "tack-on" to the school curriculum
        c. An educational reform movement
        d. A process

Think to yourself that the statement could be anything but the correct answer. This question form is more open to interpretation than other types, so read carefully and don't forget that you're answering a negative statement.

5. **Questions That Include Graphs, Tables, or Reading Passages.** As ever, read the question carefully. It likely asks for a very specific answer and not broad interpretation of the visual. Here is a simple (though not statistically accurate) example of a graph question: According to the following graph, in how many years did more men take the PRAXIS II exam than women?

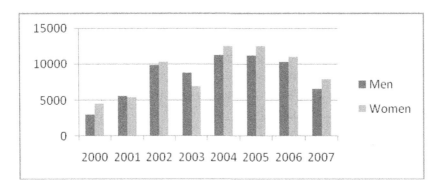

a. None
b. One
c. Two
d. Three

It may help you to simply circle the two years that answer the question. Make sure you've read the question thoroughly and once you've made your determination, double check your work. The correct answer is C.

Current Teaching Trends

Digital pedagogy and the use of 21st century teaching methods have shifted the landscape of teaching to create a bigger focus on student engagement. Student-centered classrooms now utilize technology to create efficiencies and increase digital literacy. Classrooms that once relied on memorization and the regurgitation of facts now push students to *create* and *analyze* material. The Bloom's Taxonomy chart below gives a great visual of the higher order thinking skills that current teachers are implementing in their learning objectives. There are also examples of the verbs that you might use when creating learning objectives at the assignment, course, or program level.

21st Century Bloom's Taxonomy

Lower- order			Higher- order		
Remember	Understand	Apply	Analyze	Evaluate	Create
• Define • Describe • Recall	• Classify • Explain • Summarize	• Determine • Organize • Use	• Deduct • Estimate • Outline	• Argue • Justify • Support	• Construct • Adapt • Modify

Most importantly, you'll notice that each of these verbs will allow teachers to align a specific assessment to assess the mastery of the skill that's being taught. Instead of saying "Students will learn about parts of speech," teachers will insert a measurable verb into the learning objective. The 21st century model uses S.M.A.R.T. (Specific, Measurable, Attainable, Realistic, Time-bound) assessment methods to ensure teachers can track progress and zero in on areas that students need to revisit before they have fully grasped the concept.

When reading the first objective below, you might ask yourself the following questions:

Students will:

1. Learn about parts of speech

How will they learn? How will you assess their learning? What does "learn" mean to different teachers? What does "learn" look like to different learning styles?

In this second example, the 21st century model shows specific ways students will use parts of speech.

Students will be able to:

1. Define parts of speech (lower)
2. Classify parts of speech (lower)
3. Construct a visual representation of each part of speech (higher)

Technology in the 21st Century Classroom

Student-centered classrooms now also rely heavily on technology for content delivery (PowerPoint, LMS) assessment (online quizzes) and collaborative learning (Google Drive). Particular to ESL classrooms, teachers can now record themselves speaking using lecture capture software. Students can then watch the video multiple times to ensure they've understood concepts. They have the ability to pause/rewind/replay any sections they are confused about, and they can focus on taking better notes while having the ability to watch the video a second or third time.

Online assessments also give students and teachers a better idea for comprehension level. These quick, often self-grading assessments give teachers more time to spend with students instead of grading. They eliminate human error and give teachers data needed to zero in on concepts that need to be revisited. For example, if 12 of 15 students got number 5 wrong, the teacher will know to discuss this concept in class. Online assessments may include listening, speaking, reading, and/or writing practice. This reinforces the content that was taught in the classroom and gives opportunity for practice at students' leisure. In addition, adaptable learning will help teachers by tracking user data to demonstrate learning gains. This can be completed in pre-posttest form, with conditionals within an assessment, or through small, formative assessments.

SMART Technologies, Inc. is a very popular company that creates software and hardware for educational environments. You may have heard of a "SmartBoard" before. These are promethean boards (interactive whiteboards) and are most commonly gained using grant money. They can be used as a projector for PowerPoints, their speakers can be used for audio practice, and their video options can allow you to "bring" a guest speaker into your classroom using videoconferencing, such as Skype. They record notes made on the whiteboard and record audio from lectures, which can then be saved and sent to students that were absent, or used to review for tests on varying concepts.

Google has created ample opportunity for secondary teachers in creating efficiencies for document sharing, assessment tools, and collaborative learning environments. Their drive feature can allow for easy transfer of assignment instructions, essays, and group projects. Slides can be used to create and post

PowerPoints for students to have ongoing access. Forms is a great way to create quizzes, and the data can be sorted and manipulated in a number of ways. They can also be used for self-assessment, peer evaluation, and for pre-post analyses.

As technology continues to evolve, it's critical for teachers to continue to implement tools that make their classrooms more effective and efficient while also preparing students to successfully function in a technology-driven society. Through simple lessons and technology demonstrations, students will have a great start at applying technology skills in the outside world. The classroom is a great starting place for ESL students to learn how to use technology and how to practice their own reading, writing, listening, and speaking.

Testing Tips

1. Get smart, play dumb. Sometimes a question is just a question. No one is out to trick you, so don't assume that the test writer is looking for something other than what was asked. Stick to the question as written and don't overanalyze.

2. Do a double take. Read test questions and answer choices at least twice because it's easy to miss something, to transpose a word or some letters. If you have no idea what the correct answer is, skip it and come back later if there's time. If you're still clueless, it's okay to guess. Remember, you're scored on the number of questions you answer correctly. You're not penalized for wrong answers. The worst-case scenario is that you miss a point from a good guess.

3. Turn it on its ear. The syntax of a question can often provide a clue, so make things interesting and turn the question into a statement to see if it changes the meaning or relates better (or worse) to the answer choices.

4. Get out your magnifying glass. Look for hidden clues in the questions because it's difficult to write a multiple-choice question without giving away part of the answer in the options presented. In most questions you can readily eliminate one or two potential answers, increasing your chances of answering correctly to 50/50, which will help if you've skipped a question and gone back to it (see tip #2).

5. Call it intuition. Often your first instinct is correct. If you've been studying the content you've likely absorbed something and have subconsciously retained the knowledge. On questions you're not sure about, trust your instincts because a first impression is usually correct.

6. Graffiti. Sometimes it's a good idea to mark your answers directly on the test booklet and go back to fill in the optical scan sheet later. You don't get extra points for perfectly blackened ovals. If you choose to manage your test this way, be sure not to mismark your answers when you transcribe to the scan sheet.

7. Become a clock-watcher. You have a set amount of time to answer the questions. Don't get bogged down laboring over a question you're not sure about when there are ten others you could answer more readily. If you choose to follow the advice of tip #6, be sure you leave time near the end to go back and fill in the scan sheet.

Ready? Ready.

Do the Drill

No matter how prepared you feel, it's sometimes a good idea to apply Murphy's Law. So the following tips might seem silly, mundane, or obvious, but we're including them anyway.

1. Remember, you are what you eat, so bring a snack. Choose from the list of energizing foods that appears earlier in the introduction.
2. You're not too sexy for your test. Wear comfortable clothes. You'll be distracted if your belt is too tight, or if you're too cold or too hot.
3. Lie to yourself. Even if you think you're a prompt person, pretend you're not and leave plenty of time to get to the testing center. Map it out ahead of time and do a dry run if you have to. There's no need to add road rage to your list of anxieties.
4. No ticket, no test. Bring your admission ticket as well as **two** forms of identification, including one with a picture and signature. You will not be admitted to the test without these things.
5. You can't take it with you. Leave any study aids, dictionaries, notebooks, computers and the like at home. Certain tests **do** allow a scientific or four-function calculator, so check ahead of time to learn whether your test does.
6. Prepare for the desert. Any time spent on a bathroom break **cannot** be made up later, so use your judgment on the amount you eat or drink.
7. Quiet, please! Keeping your own time is a good idea, but not with a timepiece that has a loud ticker. If you use a watch, take it off and place it nearby but not so that it distracts you. Cell phones are not allowed in the test area.

To the best of our ability, the content you need to know is represented in this book and in the accompanying online resources. The rest is up to you. You can use the study and testing tips or you can follow your own methods. Either way, you can be confident that there aren't any missing pieces of information and there shouldn't be any surprises in the content of the test.

Good luck!

COMPETENCY 1.0   LANGUAGE AND LANGUAGE LEARNING

Skill 1.1   Demonstrates knowledge of current research and major theories of home/new language acquisition and of the role of the first language in language learning, the importance of promoting receptive and productive oracy and literacy, and the value of bilingualism/biliteracy

Interlanguage

Interlanguage is a strategy used by a second language learner to compensate for his/her lack of proficiency while learning a second language. It cannot be classified as L1, nor can it be classified as L2. Rather, it could almost be considered an L3, complete with its own grammar and lexicon. Interlanguage is developed by the learner in relation to the learner's experiences (both positive and negative) with the second language. Larry Selinker introduced the theory of "interlanguage" in 1972 and asserted that L2 learners rely on certain learning strategies, to compensate in this in-between period, while the learner acquires the language. The following are some of the learning strategies of which the learner makes use:

- Generalization
- Simplification of language rules
- Circumlocution

These practices create an interlanguage, which generally assists the learner in moving from one stage to the next during second language acquisition. Interlanguage, can, however, create potential pitfalls for language learners. For example, L1 interference or language transfer occurs when a learner's primary language patterns influence his/her progress in the L2. Interference most commonly affects pronunciation, grammar structures, vocabulary and semantics.

Overgeneralization occurs when the learner attempts to apply a rule across-the-board, without regard to irregular exceptions. For example, a learner is overgeneralizing when s/he attempts to apply an "ed" ending to create a past tense for an irregular verb, such as "buyed" or "swimmed." Fossilization is a term applied by Selinker to the process in which an L1 learner reaches a plateau and accepts that less-than-fluent level, which prevents the learner from achieving L2 fluency. Fossilization occurs when non-L2 forms become fixed in the interlanguage of the L2 learner. L2 learners are highly susceptible to this phenomenon during the early stages.

Selinker theorizes that a psychological structure is "awakened" when a learner begins the process of second language acquisition. He attached great significance to the notion that the learner and the native speaker would not create similar sounds if they attempted to communicate the same thought, idea, or meaning.

Markedness

Another theory respecting linguistic concepts in interlanguage analysis is the study of markedness. This puts forward the theory that some structures are more common in world languages than others. The more common structures are referred to as unmarked, whereas marked structures are those that are not common. For example, in the word pair happy/unhappy, 'unhappy' is marked because it is a morphologically negative form of the unmarked' happy'. In the word pair old/young, old is unmarked because of its use in a question i.e. "How old are you?" rather than, "How young are you?".

One hypothesis that emerged from this theory is that the less marked structures are acquired earlier than more marked structures. However, other studies have concluded that L2 learners are more likely to acquire a marked structure with frequent input than an unmarked structure that is not used frequently. Furthermore, research has pointed out the role of L1 transfer in this area. It has been suggested that learners might be able to transfer unmarked structures from their L1 more readily than marked structures.

Universal Grammar/Language and Chomsky

Chomsky put forward the theory of Universal Grammar (UG), which assumes that all languages have a common structural basis or set of rules. Chomsky based this on his research on L1 acquisition by children. He observed that the input to which children are exposed is insufficient for them to learn the rules of their target language. Therefore, he hypothesized that these children must rely on some innate knowledge of language structures in order to acquire their respective L1. Recently, there has been some controversy about the validity of this theory.

There are additional controversies in theories of new language acquisition relating to the age of the language learner. The critical period hypothesis states that there is a period during language acquisition when learners are able to achieve native-like proficiency in the target language. Studies show that L2 learners who begin learning as adults are often unable to achieve native-like ability in pronunciation. This could be a result of social conditions, in which L1 learners have a lot of opportunity to interact in their first language.

Krashen's Five Principles

Another set of home/new language theories is based on Stephen Krashen's research. Most people understand his theories based on five principles:

1. Acquisition-Learning hypothesis: There is a difference between learning a language and acquiring it. Children acquire a first language easily—it's a natural process based on frequent interactions. But adults often have to learn a language through coursework, studying, and memorizing. One can acquire a second language, but often it requires more deliberate and natural interaction within that language.

2. Monitor hypothesis: The learned language monitors the acquired language. In other words, this is when a person's "grammar check" kicks in and keeps awkward, incorrect language out of a person's L2 communication.

3. Natural order hypothesis: This theory suggests that learning grammatical structures is predictable and follows a natural order.

4. Input hypothesis: Some people call this comprehensible input. This means that a language learner will learn best when the instruction or conversation is just above the learner's ability. That way, the learner has the foundation to understand most of the language, but will still have to figure out, often in context, what that last, more difficult, element means.

5. Affective filter hypothesis: This theory suggests that people will learn a second language when they are relaxed, have high levels of motivation, and have a decent level of self-confidence.

The above discussion shows the importance of analyzing English Language Learners' native languages as well as an understanding the linguistic concepts of the target language in order to recognize the different stages of L2 development within a classroom. It is important for ESOL teachers to try to introduce new materials based on this analysis and to provide learners with appropriate learning strategies that will help them achieve native-like proficiency in the target language.

Chomsky: Language Acquisition Device
Chomsky's theory, described as Nativist, asserts that humans are born with a special biological brain mechanism, called a Language Acquisition Device (LAD). His theory supposes that the ability to learn language is innate, that nature is more important than nurture, and that experience using language is only necessary in order to activate the LAD. Critics point out that Chomsky's LAD theory underestimates the influence that cognition and language have on each other's development.

Piaget: Cognitive Constructivism
Piaget's central interest is children's cognitive development. Piaget argues that learning is a process of active discovery and knowledge is something that is actively constructed; that the best learning takes place when students are provided with opportunities to play, to practice, to scaffold and to cognitively process what they are learning. For Piaget, skill and drill techniques are not effective methods for real learning and knowledge acquisition.

Vygotsky: Social Constructivism and Language
Vygotsky's central focus is the relationship between the developments of thought and language in the ways that different languages impact a person's thinking. He suggests that what Piaget saw as young children's egocentric speech was actually private speech, the child's way of using words to think about something, which progressed from social speech to thinking in words. Vygotsky views language first as social communication, which gradually promotes both language itself and cognition.

Intentionality

Some contemporary researchers and theorists criticize earlier theories and suggest children, their behaviors, and their attempts to understand and communicate are misunderstood when the causes of language development are thought to be either outside the child or mechanistically within the child's brain. They recognize that children are active learners who co-construct their worlds and that language development is part of their holistic development, emerging from cognitive, emotional, and social interactions. They believe language development depends on the child's social and cultural environment, the people in it, and their interactions. How children represent these factors in their minds is fundamental to language development. They believe a child's agenda and the interactions generated by the child promote language learning. The adult's role, actions, and speech are still considered important, but adults need to be able to "mind read" and adjust their side of the co-construction to relate to an individual child's understanding and interpretation.

Theories about language development help us see that enjoying "proto conversations" with children (treating them as people who can understand, share and have intentions in sensitive interchanges) and truly listening to young children are effective ways to promote language development.

Brain research has shown that a crucial factor affecting language acquisition is the onset of puberty. Before puberty, a person uses one area of the brain for language learning; after puberty, a different area of the brain is used. A person who begins to learn a second language after the onset of puberty will likely find language learning more difficult and depend more on repetition.

Some researchers have focused on analyzing aspects of the language to be acquired. Factors they consider include:

- error analysis: recognizing patterns of errors
- interlanguage: analyzing what aspects of the target language are universal
- developmental patterns: the order in which features of a language are acquired and the sequence in which a specific feature is acquired.

Teaching English Language Learners poses some unique challenges, particularly in a standards-based environment. Teachers should teach with the student's developmental level in mind. Different approaches should be used to ensure that these students get multiple opportunities to learn and practice English and still learn content.

Bilingualism and Biliteracy

ESOL teachers are expected to demonstrate knowledge of the value of bilingualism and biliteracy. In New York state districts and schools, students can earn a Seal of Biliteracy, along with their high school diplomas. In order to do this, schools provide all learners with "opportunities to participate in language learning or language support programs that lead to proficiency in English and other languages," including students' home languages.

For more information on these opportunities and other strategies to help ELLs succeed, click on a PDF link to download the NYSED's Blueprint for English Language Learner Success at this website: (http://www.nysed.gov/common/nysed/files/programs/bilingual-ed/nysblueprintforellsuccess.2016.pdf)

Skill 1.2   Demonstrates knowledge of social, academic and discipline-specific language uses, and understands the importance of the English Language Learners' simultaneous development of basic communication and academic English language skills

Academic discourse refers to formal academic learning. This includes all four core skills: listening, reading, speaking, and writing. Academic learning is important in order for students to succeed in school. Cummins differentiated between two types of language proficiency: basic interpersonal communication skills (BICS) and cognitive academic language proficiency (CALP). According to research, an average student can acquire BICS within two to five years of language learning whereas CALP can take from four to seven years. A lot of factors are involved in the acquisition of CALP, such as age, language proficiency level, literacy in the first language, etc.

Academic discourse not only includes the knowledge of content-area vocabulary but also the knowledge of various skills and strategies that are essential to successfully complete academic tasks in a mainstream classroom. It includes skills such as inferring, classifying, analyzing, synthesizing, and evaluating. Textbooks used in a classroom require abstract thinking where the information is context-reduced. As students reach higher grades, they are required to think critically and apply new knowledge to solve problems.

Additionally, the language of academic discourse is also complex for English language learners. With respect to reading and writing, use of complex grammatical structures is frequently found in academic discourse, which makes it challenging for the language learner. Also, passive voice is normally used in science and other subject area textbooks. Similarly, the use of reference, pronouns, modals, etc., is a common feature of academic discourse which might cause problems for ESL learners. All of these language features of academic discourse help to convey the intended meaning of the author. Therefore, it is necessary to explicitly teach these language features of the text to the students in order for them to become skilled readers and writers.

Genre is also an important aspect of academic discourse. Different genres employ styles of writing that are unique. The organization of a text structure differs according to the purpose of the author – for example, mystery versus romance. Likewise, in academic reading students come across multiple texts that vary in organization and style according to the purpose of the author and the audience in question. Students need to realize the different features of multiple texts to be efficient readers. With respect to writing, students need to determine the purpose of their writing – for example, argumentative writing versus story writing.

In short, explicit instruction of social, academic and discipline-specific language skills, grammar and vocabulary, should be provided to the students to help them develop basic communication and academic English language skills in order to succeed in a school setting.

Skill 1.3   Demonstrates knowledge of stages and sequences in second-language acquisition

L1 and L2 learning follows many, if not all, of the same steps.

- Pre Production: The learner knows less than approximately 500 receptive words and does not produce speech. The absence of speech does not indicate a lack of learning and teachers should not try to force the learner to speak. Having the learner point, draw, mime or nod can check comprehension; this is also known as the Receptive or Silent stage.

- Early Production: The learner knows about 1,000 receptive words and can produce one- or two-word phrases, present-tense verbs and some key phrases and words. The learner can understand and respond to simple questions and yes/no, either/or prompts. Also known as the Private Speech stage.

- Speech Emergence: The learner knows about 3,000 receptive words and can communicate using short phrases and sentences. Long sentences typically have grammatical errors. Also known as the Lexical Chunks stage.

- Intermediate Fluency: The learner knows about 6,000 receptive words and begins to make complex statements, state opinions, ask for clarification, share thoughts, and speak at greater length. Also known as the Formulaic Speech stage.

- Advanced Language Proficiency: The learner develops a good level of fluency and can make semantic and grammatical generalizations. Also known as the Experimental or Simplified Speech stage.

Understanding that students must go through a predictable, sequential series of stages helps teachers to recognize the student's progress and respond effectively. Providing comprehensible input will help students advance their language learning at any stage.

Skill 1.4   Demonstrates knowledge of the transferability of first- language literacy skills into English

In some ways, we only learn to read once. Once we figure out how reading works in our native language, we can apply the same skills to a new language. Learning to read in a new language with a similar orthographic system (e.g., Spanish and English) is easier than learning to read in a language with a totally different system of writing (such as Mandarin), but the skills are similar. It is important for ELLs to increase their vocabulary and knowledge of the structure of English, their new language. By building on what the ELL already knows with regards to literacy, language, and experiences in his or her native language, teachers will be able to improve the reading level of the ELL in English. For this reason, it is necessary to evaluate the ELL in his or her first, native, or heritage language in order to initiate the best reading instruction in English.

Teachers can also use the similarities and differences of the different languages to teach learning strategies. For example, the adjective usually comes before the noun in English but in Spanish it more frequently comes after the noun. Drawing attention to this difference can help Spanish speakers build comprehension skills. A text written in English is expected to have a clear main idea and several supporting details to explain or support it. Other languages are more descriptive and depend on the beauty of the language to convey the writer's meaning. By using the concept of cognates, both true and false, teachers can improve vocabulary development.

Schumm (2006) emphasizes that not only are the reading level characteristics important, but also the differences between L1 and L2, because these may influence the assumed level of the student. Some of the questions she proposes to elicit these similarities and differences provide further evaluation of reading level characteristics:

- Is the L1 writing system logographic like Mandarin, syllabic like Cherokee, or alphabetic like English and Greek?
- How does the L1 syntax compare with the L2 syntax?
- Are the spelling patterns phonetic with consistent grapheme-phoneme relationships (e.g., Spanish or French) or are there multiple vowel sounds (e.g., English)?
- Do students read from left to right and top to bottom in their L1?
- Are there true cognates (Spanish instrucción and English instruction) and false cognates (Spanish librería <bookstore> and English library) that will help or confuse the ELL?
- Are the discourse patterns and writing styles of L1 and L2 similar or different?
- Does the L1 writing style emphasize directness in an argument, with main ideas supported by convincing details? Or does it employ a less direct style that seeks to show a reader a point of view.

Taking these questions into consideration helps the ESOL teacher to more accurately assess and support English Language Learners.

Skill 1.5 **Demonstrates knowledge of the learning processes (e.g., metacognitive and cognitive strategies) that are involved in internalizing language rules for second language acquisition**

Cognitive strategies

Cognitive strategies are vital to second language acquisition; their most salient feature is the manipulation of the new language. The following are the most basic strategies: "Practicing," "Receiving and Sending Messages," "Analyzing and Reasoning," and "Creating Structure for Input and Output," which can be remembered by the acronym, "PRAC."

- Practicing: The following strategies promote the learner's grasp of the language: practice, constant repetition, make attempts to imitate a native speaker's accent, concentrate on sounds, and practice in a realistic setting.

- Receiving and Sending Messages: These strategies help the learner quickly locate key points and then interpret the meaning: skim through information to determine "need to know" vs. "nice to know," use available resources (print and non-print) for receiving and sending messages.

- Analyzing and Reasoning: Use general rules to understand the meaning and then work into specifics, and break down unfamiliar expressions into parts.

- Creating Structure for Input and Output: Choose a format for taking meaningful notes, practice summarizing long passages, and use highlighters as a way to focus on main ideas or important specific details.

Metacognitive Strategies

The ESOL teacher is responsible for helping students become aware of their own individual learning strategies and for helping them constantly improve those strategies and add to them. Each student should have his/her own toolbox of skills for planning, managing, and evaluating the language-learning process.

- Centering Your Learning: Review a key concept or principle and link it to already existing knowledge. Make a firm decision to pay attention to the general concept, ignore input that is distracting, and learn skills in the proper order.

- Arranging and Planning Your Learning: The following strategies help the learner maximize the learning experience: take the time to understand how a language is learned; create optimal learning conditions, i.e., regulate noise, lighting and temperature; obtain the appropriate books, etc.; and set reasonable long-term and short-term goals.

- Evaluate Your Learning: The following strategies help learners assess their learning achievements: keep track of errors that hinder advancement, and keep track of progress, e.g., reading faster now than last month.

Socioaffective Strategies

Affective strategies are those that help the learner to control the emotions and attitudes that hinder progress in learning the second language and at the same time to learn to interact in a social environment. Socioaffective strategies are broken down into affective and social strategies. There are three sets of affective strategies: "Lowering Your Anxiety," "Encouraging Yourself," and "Taking Your Emotional Temperature," which are easily remembered with the acronym LET.

- Lowering Your Anxiety: These strategies try to maintain emotional equilibrium with physical activities. Use meditation and/or deep breathing to relax, listen to calming music, read a funny book, or watch a comedy.

- Encourage Yourself: These strategies help support and self-motivate the learner. Stay positive through self-affirmations. Take risks, and give yourself rewards.

- Take Your Emotional Temperature: These strategies help learners control their emotions by understanding what they are feeling emotionally, as well as why they are feeling that way. Listen to body signals; create a checklist to keep track of feelings and motivations during the second-language-acquisition process; keep a diary to record progress and feelings; and share feelings with a classmate or friend.

Social strategies affect how the learner interacts in a social setting. The following are three useful strategies for interacting socially: asking questions; cooperating with others; and empathizing with others. These can be remembered by the acronym ACE.

- Ask Questions: Ask for clarification or help. Request that the speaker slow down, repeat, paraphrase, etc., and ask to be corrected.

- Cooperate with Others: Interact with more than one person; work cooperatively with a partner or small group; and work with a native speaker of the language.

- Empathize with Others: Learn how to relate to others, remembering that people usually have more aspects in common than differences. Empathize with another student by learning about his/her culture and being aware and sensitive to the thoughts and feelings of others. Understanding and emphasizing will help that student, but it will also help the empathizer.

Skill 1.6	Demonstrates understanding of the five distinct levels of English language proficiency defined by the New York State Education Department (entering, emerging, transitioning, expanding, commanding)

In New York State, if newly enrolled students, after completing a home language questionnaire and participating in an interview with a school representative, are identified as speaking a language other than English in the home environment, they will be required to take the New York State Identification Test for English Language Learners (NYSITELL). Schools use the results of this test to assess students' English Language proficiency levels.

New York State has five English Language Proficiency levels: Entering, Emerging, Transitioning, Expanding and Commanding.

If a student scores below Commanding on the test, s/he is considered to be an English Language Learner and receives either Bilingual Education (BE) or English as a New Language (ENL) services. The assessment helps guide instruction and helps identify students' English Language Learners' strengths and challenges in receptive and productive skills (reading, listening, speaking, and writing).

- A student at the Entering level needs substantial support and structure in English language learning because s/he struggles to demonstrate English language proficiency in academic contexts.

- A student at the Emerging level is still largely dependent on support and structure in her/his learning and is not yet proficient in academic contexts.

- A student at the Transitioning level is more independent and needs less support but still has not yet become proficient in English in academic contexts.

- At the Expanding level of proficiency, students are increasingly able to be more independent and are clearly approaching the English Language proficiency level necessary to function well in various academic contexts.

- Finally, at the Commanding level, a student is proficient in the English Language in various academic contexts and, therefore, is not an ELL.

Students' proficiency levels and test scores also help the school to determine the optimal number of minutes of English Language instruction for each English Language Learner.

Skill 1.7   Demonstrates knowledge of sociolinguistic concepts (e.g., dialect diversity in English, intercultural differences in communication styles, code switching)

American English language usage is influenced by the social and regional situation of its users. Linguists have found that speakers adapt pronunciation, vocabulary, grammar and sentence structure depending on the social situation. For example, the decision to use –ing or –in at the end of a present participle depends on the formality of the situation. Speakers talking with their friends will often drop the "g" and use –in which signals that the situation is more informal and relaxed. These variations are also related to factors such as age, gender, education, socioeconomic status, and personality (and combinations of these factors).

We call this type of shift a change in register, how language is used in a particular setting or for a particular purpose. People change their speech register depending on such sociolinguistic variables as:

- Formality of situation
- Attitude towards topic
- Attitude towards listeners
- Relation of speaker to others

Changing speech registers may be completely subconscious for native speakers. For example, if a university professor takes her car in for servicing, the manner and speech she uses to communicate with the mechanic will probably differ significantly from the manner and speech she uses to deliver a lecture. If she were to use a formal tone and academic vocabulary, the mechanic might feel like she was being treated as a student rather than a professional or she might not understand the academic jargon the professor is using. Likewise, when the mechanic explains the mechanical diagnosis, she most likely chooses a simplified vocabulary rather than using completely technical language, or jargon, that the professor wouldn't understand. When speakers use jargon from a field unfamiliar to the listener, it can make the listener feel insecure, and perhaps feel that the speaker does not respect him/her.

There are five basic types of language registers:

1. Static: Formal language that rarely changes e.g. laws, the Pledge of Allegiance
2. Formal: Formal language that is usually one way communication e.g. lecture, judges' rulings, speeches
3. Consultative: The consultative register consists of a structured form of communication that generally guides communicative interactions between speakers and listeners e.g. lawyers and clients, doctors and patients, teachers and students.
4. Casual: The casual register is the language we use with peers, friends and family members. It is less formal, less structured, and may use language specific to the group that is interacting.
5. Intimate: The intimate language register tends to be private and only used within the context of close family members, friends and partners.

Although speakers can easily transition from one adjacent level to another, it is unusual and sometimes seen as offensive when speakers skip one or more levels.

Code-switching refers to a switch between languages or the combination of elements of different languages within one conversation. This can be a function of limited proficiency (as speakers may not have the skills to express some ideas) or of advanced proficiency (as speakers find one language more useful for expressing certain concepts or ideas than others). In an academic context, code-switching is generally not appropriate but has great creative potential.

ESOL teachers should be aware of these sociolinguistic functions of language and compare different social functions of language with their students. Knowing and being able to use appropriate registers allows learners to function more effectively in social situations. Learners must acquire the social as well as the linguistic aspects of American English. Sociolinguistic functions of a language are best acquired by using the language in authentic situations.

Sociolinguistic diversity, which is language variations based on regional and social differences, affects teachers' language attitudes and practices. Teachers must respect the validity of any group's or individual's language patterns, while at the same time teaching standard English. Vernacular versions of English have well-established patterns and rules to support them. Making learners aware of language variations leads to increased interest in language learning and better ability to switch among one or more registers or dialects and standard English.

ELLs tend to adapt linguistic structures to their familiar culture, modifying specific concepts and practices. Teachers must identify these variations, call attention to them, and teach the standard English equivalent. The goal is not to eliminate linguistic diversity, but rather to enable learners to control their language use so that they can willfully use standard English in addition to their cultural variation.

Various functional adaptations of English have great significance to the cultural groups that use them. Attempting to eliminate variations is not only futile, but raises hostility and reluctance to learn English. Stable, socially shared structures emerge from the summed effects of many individual communication practices. Firmly ingrained language patterns serve a purpose within the community that uses them.

Unique variations can arise in as limited a spectrum as a school. New non-standard English words can represent a particular group's identity, or function as a means to solidify social relationships. As long as students recognize that a variation should not be used as if it were standard English, there should be no problem with its use.

Skill 1.8 **Demonstrates knowledge of the relationship between language and culture and how this can affect English Language acquisition, and strategies to help students recognize differences between home culture and language and the school culture and language**

It is important for ESOL teachers and English Language Learners to understand the strong connection between language and culture. Language is used to explain, express and develop culture, and cultural practices are often rooted in language specific to the cultural group(s). Language and culture are intertwined. When learning English as a new language, students are also learning about a new culture. Teachers can help students by applying this understanding to instruction and by helping students become aware of the ways in which they are learning a language and learning about a culture(s).

Some ways to do this include: being empathetic with the attitudes English Language Learners may bring to class that differ from the L2 culture, actively teaching about cultural aspects while teaching English, maintaining a respectful classroom environment that can observe differences while encouraging all students to celebrate and value diversity.

Skill 1.9 **Demonstrates knowledge of current theories and research in literacy development; recognizes the importance of schema theory in reading instruction and of the interrelationship between decoding and comprehension in English; understands the importance of recognizing and encouraging students to build on their prior knowledge and experience; and understands the different elements (e.g., phonemic awareness, vocabulary, comprehension) of literacy development**

Schema
Schemata need to be activated to draw upon the previous knowledge and learning of the English Language Learner. The use of graphics to encourage pre-reading thought about a topic (e.g., brainstorming, web maps, and organizational charts) activates this knowledge and shows how information is organized in the students' minds. Schumm (2006) states that research has shown:

- More prior knowledge permits a reader to understand and remember more (Brown, Bransford, Ferrara, & Campione, 1983).
- Prior knowledge must be activated to improve comprehension (Bransford & Johnson, 1972).
- Failure to activate prior knowledge is one cause of poor readers (Paris & Lindauer, 1976).
- Good readers may reject ideas that conflict with their prior knowledge (Pressley, 2000).

The research on schema has important implications for instruction and academic and social success of English Language Learners. For example, ESOL teachers need to understand that when introducing a lesson, students need to be engaged. They need to know that the material they will be learning in the lesson is interesting and important. They need to be given a reason to motivate themselves to learn it.

Students also need to know what they are going to study—they need to know what they are expected to learn. The lesson objectives and teacher expectations should be clear from the start of the lesson. Finally, when introducing a lesson, if English Language Learners are able to make connections between existing knowledge and new knowledge throughout the lesson, they will be more successful in retaining and utilizing the new knowledge.

Decoding and Comprehension

Teaching decoding skills is considered one of the effective methods of reading instruction. The emphasis is on teaching the phoneme-grapheme correspondences. In order to develop effective reading skills, students should aim for automaticity-- i.e., the process of decoding letter-sounds becomes automatic. This leads to fluent reading where the brain may process many letters, sounds, and words at the same time. Automaticity is positively related to students' achievement in reading, as once decoding skills are mastered, more attention can be given to understanding the overall meaning of a phrase or sentence (comprehension). Even when English Language Learners can decode English, they will continue to benefit from explicit instruction in developing strategies to improve their comprehension skills.

Teaching decoding skills is considered one of the effective methods of reading instruction. The emphasis is on teaching the phoneme-grapheme correspondences. In order to develop effective reading skills, students should aim for automaticity-- i.e., the brain process of decoding letter sounds becomes automatic. This leads to fluent reading where the brain may process many letters, sounds, and words at the same time. This is positively related to students' achievement in reading, as once decoding skill is mastered, more attention can be given to mastering the overall meaning of a phrase or sentence (comprehension). However, students still need explicit instruction in developing strategies to improve their comprehension skills.

Phonics and other linguistic approaches to teaching reading are important in terms of word identification skills. Accurate and rapid word recognition skill leads to fluency in reading, which is considered one of the five critical components of the reading process (National Reading Panel). When the reader's decoding skills become automatic, s/he is able to focus attention on constructing meaning. For readers who have not yet reached automaticity of decoding skills, reading is a slow, laborious process. Fluent readers are more likely to engage in extensive reading as compared to struggling readers. The view that if readers read more, they will achieve fluency is not always applicable for ESL learners. Expert teacher guidance is necessary for these learners to reach fluency. Several studies have focused on the type of instruction that would increase fluency in readers. These instructional practices include:

- modeled reading
- repeated reading of familiar text
- independent reading
- coached reading of appropriately selected materials
- chunking of text
- word reading practice

Even though fluency is an important part of reading, it is in itself not sufficient to ensure high levels of reading achievement and comprehension. Fluency is based on a foundation of oral language skills, phonemic awareness, familiarity with letter forms, and efficient decoding skills. In short, a combination of instruction in decoding and reading comprehension is required for students to achieve high levels of reading skill.

Skill 1.10 **Applies knowledge of phonetics and phonology (e.g., distinguishing among classes of sound), English morphology and lexicon, syntactic features (e.g., a verb phrase), discourse features (e.g., cohesion), and the structure of the English language to support English language development**

Phonetics and Phonology

The definition of phonology can be summarized as "the way in which speech sounds form patterns" (Díaz-Rico & Weed, 1995). Phonology is a subset of the linguistics field, which studies the organization and systems of sound within a particular language.

When babies babble or make what we call "baby talk," they are actually experimenting with all of the sounds represented in all languages. As they learn a specific language, they become more proficient in the sounds of that language and forget how to make sounds that they don't need or use.

Phonemes, pitch, and stress are all components of phonology. Because each affects the meaning of communications, they are variables that ELLs must recognize and learn.

Phonology analyzes the sound structure of the given language by:

- determining which phonetic sounds have the most significance
- explaining how these sounds influence a native speaker of the language

For example, the Russian alphabet has a consonant, which, when pronounced, sounds like the soft 'g' sound from the word "rouge" in French. English speakers typically have difficulty pronouncing this sound pattern, because inherently they know this is not a typical English sound--even though it occasionally is encountered (Díaz-Rico & Weed, 1995).

Mastering a sound that does not occur in the learner's first language requires ongoing repetition, both of hearing the sound and attempting to say it. The older the learner, the more difficult this becomes, especially if the learner has only spoken one language before reaching puberty. Correct pronunciation may literally require years of practice because initially the learner may not hear the sound correctly. Expecting an ELL to master a foreign pronunciation quickly leads to frustration for the teacher and the learner. With enough focused repetition, and listening and speaking practice, the learner may eventually hear the difference and then be able to imitate it.

A phoneme is the smallest unit of sound that affects meaning. In English, there are approximately 44 speech sounds yet only 26 letters, so the sounds, when combined, become words. For this reason, English is not considered a phonetic language with one-to-one correspondence between letters and sounds. For example, consider the two words, "pin" and "bin." The only difference is the first consonant of the words, the "p" in "pin" and "b" in "bin." This makes the sounds "p" and "b" phonemes in English, because the difference in sound creates a difference in meaning.

Focusing on phonemes to provide pronunciation practice allows students to have fun while they learn to recognize and say sounds. Pairs or groups of words that have a set pattern make learning easier. For example, students can practice saying or thinking of words that rhyme but begin with a different phoneme, such as tan, man, fan, and ran. Other groups of words might start with the same phoneme followed by various vowel sounds, such as ten, ton, tan, and tin. This kind of alliteration can be expanded into tongue twisters that students find challenging and fun. Vowels and consonants should be introduced in a deliberate order to allow combinations that form real words.

Pitch and Stress
Pitch in communication plays a role in determining the context or meaning of a series of words. A string of words can communicate more than one meaning – for example, when posed as a question or statement. For instance, the phrase "I can't go" acts as a statement, if the pitch or intonation falls. However, the same phrase becomes the question "I can't go?" if the pitch or intonation rises for the word "go."

Stress can occur at a word or sentence level. At the word level, different stresses on the syllable can actually modify the word's meaning. Consider the word "conflict." To pronounce it as a noun, one would stress the first syllable, as in "CONflict." However, to use it as a verb, the second syllable would be stressed, as in "conFLICT."

Different dialects sometimes pronounce the same word differently, even though both pronunciations have the same meaning. For example, in some parts of the United States the word "insurance" is pronounced by stressing the second syllable, while in other parts of the country the first syllable is stressed.

At the sentence level, stress can also be used to vary the meaning. For example, consider the following questions and how the meaning changes, according to the stressed words:

> *He* did that? (Emphasis is on the person)
> He *did* that? (Emphasis is on the action)
> He did *that*? (Emphasis is on the object of the action)

This type of meaning differentiation is difficult for most ELL students to grasp and requires innovative teaching, such as acting out the three different meanings. Since pitch and stress can change the meaning of a sentence completely, students must learn to recognize these differences in order to develop proficiency in English Language speaking and listening skills.

Morphology and Morphemes
Unlike languages such as Spanish or French, English has multiple pronunciations of vowels and consonants, which contributes to making it a difficult language to learn.

Morphology refers to the process of how the words of a language are formed to create meaningful messages. ESOL teachers need to be aware of the principles of morphology in English to provide meaningful activities that will help in the process of language acquisition.

Morphemic analysis requires breaking a word down into its component parts to determine its meaning. It shows the relationship between the root or base word and the prefix and/or suffix to determine the word's meaning.

A morpheme is the smallest unit of language system which has meaning. These units are more commonly known as: the root word, the prefix, and the suffix. They cannot be broken down into smaller units.

1. The root word or base word is the key to understanding a word, because this is where the actual meaning is determined.
2. A prefix is a syllable or syllables appearing in front of the root or base word which alters the meaning of the root or base word.
3. A suffix is a letter or letters added to the end of the word which alter the original tense or meaning of the root or base word.

The following is an example of how morphemic analysis can be applied to a word:

1. Choose a root or base word, such as "kind."
2. Create as many new words as possible, by changing the prefix and suffix.
3. New words would include unkind, kindness, and kindly.

Learning common roots, prefixes, and suffixes greatly helps ELLs to decode unfamiliar words. This learning can make a big difference in how well a student understands written language. Students who can decode unfamiliar words become less frustrated when reading in English and, as a result, are likely to read more. They have greater comprehension and their language skills improve more quickly. Providing English Language Learners with the tools to decode unfamiliar words also enables them to perform better on standardized tests because they are more likely to understand the questions and answer choices.

Guessing at the meaning of words (using knowledge of morphemes) should be encouraged. Too often, students become dependent on translation dictionaries, which causes the students not to develop morphemic analysis skills. Practice should include identifying roots, prefixes, and suffixes, as well as using morphemic knowledge to form new words.

ESOL learners need to understand the structure of words in English, and how words may be created and altered. Some underlying principles of the morphology of English are:

1. Morphemes may be free and able to stand by themselves (e.g., chair, bag) or they may be bound or derivational, needing other morphemes to create meaning (e.g., un-kind, en-able).

2. Knowledge of the meanings of derivational morphemes such as prefixes and suffixes enables students to decode word meanings and create words in the language through word analysis, e.g., un-happy means not happy.
3. Some morphemes in English provide grammatical rather than semantic information for words and sentences (e.g., of, the, and).
4. Words can be combined in English to create new compound words (e.g., key + chain = keychain).

ESOL teachers also need to be aware that principles of morphology from the native language may be transferred to either promote or interfere with the second language learning process.

Sentence Structures

A sentence is a group of words that has a subject and predicate, and expresses a complete idea. A subject tells us what or whom the sentence is about and the predicate makes a statement about what the subject is or does. Subjects and predicates can be modified and combined in different ways to make simple, compound or complex sentences. [In all the following examples, subjects are underlined and predicates italicized.]

> Example: The snow *falls quietly.*

Subject: The subject, or the topic of a sentence, consists of a noun or a pronoun and all the words that modify it. "The snow" is the subject in the above example. The simple subject is the main part of the subject. "Snow" is the simple subject.

Predicate: The predicate makes a statement or a comment about the subject and it consists of a verb and all the words that modify it; "falls quietly" is the predicate in the above example. The simple predicate is the main part of the predicate and is always the verb; "falls" is the simple predicate.

Compound subject: a subject consisting of two or more pronouns, e.g., Books and magazines *filled the room.*

Compound predicate: a predicate that contains more than one verb pertaining to the subject, e.g., The boys *walked and talked.*

Sentences in English are of three types:

Simple Sentence: A simple sentence, or independent clause, is a complete thought consisting of a single subject and a single predicate:

> The bus *was late.*

Compound Sentence: A compound sentence consists of two independent clauses joined together by a coordinator (and, or, nor, but, for, yet, so):

> <u>Tom</u> *walked to the bus station* and <u>he</u> *took the bus*.

Complex Sentence: A complex sentence is a sentence consisting of a dependent clause (a group words with a subject and predicate that are not a complete thought) and an independent clause joined together using a subordinator (although, after, when, because, since, while):

> After I write the report, <u>I</u> *will submit it to my teacher*.

Sentences serve different purposes. They can make a statement (declarative), ask a question (interrogative), give a command (imperative), or express a sense of urgency (exclamatory). Understanding the different purposes for sentences can help ELLs understand the relationship between what they write and the ideas they want to express.

ELLs often over-generalize that sentence fragments are short and complete sentences are long. When they truly understand what constitutes a sentence, they will realize that length has nothing to do with whether a sentence is complete or not. For example:

> "He ran." is a complete sentence.
> "After the very funny story began" is a fragment

To make these distinctions, learners must know the parts of speech and understand the difference between independent clauses, dependent clauses, and phrases.

Phrase: a group of words that does not have a subject and a predicate and cannot stand alone. The most common types of phrases are prepositional (in the room); participial (walking down the street); and infinitive (to run).

Parts of speech: the eight classifications for words. Each part of speech has a specific role in sentences. This can be quite difficult for ELLs because the same word can have a different role in different sentences, and a different meaning entirely. Identifying the subject and predicate of the sentence helps to distinguish what role a particular word plays in a sentence. Since English is generally a subject-verb-object language, the placement of a word in a sentence relative to the subject or verb indicates what part of speech it is.

- That TV show was boring.
- I will show you my new dress.
- The band plays show tunes at half-time.

In these examples, the word show is first a noun, then a verb, and finally an adjective.

The parts of speech include:

Noun: a person, place, thing or idea. Common nouns are non-specific, while proper nouns name a particular person, place, thing, or idea, and are capitalized.

Verb: an action or state of being.

Pronoun: a word that takes the place of a noun.

Personal pronouns can be:

- first, second, or third person (I, you, he, she, it);
- singular or plural (I/we, you/you, he, she, it/they); and
- subjective or objective (I/me, you/you, he/him, she/her, it/it, we/us, they/them).

Possessive pronouns show ownership (my, mine, your, yours, his, her, hers, its, our, ours, your, yours, their, and theirs).

Indefinite pronouns refer to persons, places, things or ideas in general, such as any, each, both, most, something.

Adjective: a word that modifies a noun or pronoun. Adjectives answer questions such as What kind? How many? and Which?

Adverb: a word that modifies a verb, and adjective, or another adverb. Adverbs answer the questions How? When? Where? How often? and To what extent?

Prepositions: occur in a phrase with a noun or pronoun and show the relationship between a noun or pronoun and another word in a sentence. They describe, or show location, direction, or time. Prepositional phrases can have as few as two words, but can include any number or adjectives.

Interjection: a word that shows surprise or strong feeling. It can stand alone (Help!) or be used within a sentence (Oh no, I forgot my wallet!)

Constructing sentences involves combining words in grammatically correct ways to communicate the desired thought. Avoiding fragments and run-ons requires continual sentence analysis. The test of a complete sentence is: Does it contain a subject, a predicate and express a complete idea? Providing opportunities for English Language Learners to practice identifying independent clauses, dependent clauses, and phrases helps them master the skill of writing complete sentences.

Syntax

Syntax involves the order in which words are arranged to create meaning. Different languages use different patterns for sentence structures. Syntax also refers to the rules for creating correct sentence patterns. English, like many other languages, is a subject-verb-object language, which means that in most sentences the subject precedes the verb, and the object follows the verb. ELLs whose native language follows a subject-verb-object pattern will find it easier to master English syntax.

The process of second language acquisition includes forming generalizations about the new language and internalizing the rules that are observed. During the Preproduction or Silent period, before learners attempt verbal communication, they are engaged in the process of building a set of syntactic rules for creating grammatically correct sentences in the second language. We don't yet fully understand the nature of this process, but we do know that learners must go through this process of observing, drawing conclusions about language constructs, and testing the validity of their conclusions. This is why learners benefit more from intense language immersion than from error correction.

Language acquisition is a gradual, hierarchical, and cumulative process. This means that learners must go through and master each stage in sequence, much as Piaget theorized for learning in general. In terms of syntax, this means learners must acquire specific grammatical structures, first recognizing the difference between subject and predicate; putting subject before predicate; and learning more complex variations, such as questions, negatives, and relative clauses.

While learners must pass through each stage and accumulate the language skills learned in each progressive level, learners use different approaches to mastering these skills. Some learners use more cognitive processing procedures, which means their learning takes place more through thought processes. Other learners tend to use psycholinguistic procedures, learning more through speech. Regardless of how learners process information, they all proceed through the same stages from simple to more complex and sophisticated syntax.

Each progressive step requires the learner to use knowledge from the previous step, as well as new knowledge of the language. As ELLs progress to more advanced stages of syntax, they may react differently, depending on their ability to acquire the new knowledge required for mastery. A learner who successfully integrates the new knowledge makes generalizations, eliminates erroneous conclusions, and increasingly uses syntactical rules correctly. Some learners may struggle with the higher syntactic levels and may revert to syntactical rules learned at easier stages and fail to integrate the new knowledge. When patterns of errors reflect lower level stages, the ESOL teacher should re-teach the new syntactical stage in order to help the learners become proficient.

Cohesion is related to the way meaning is maintained in different parts of a text or conversation. In many ways it can be compared to the way context includes essential background information that enables understanding even when certain elements are omitted. For example, in a story, the writer may at times leave out the character's name and instead use pronouns (she, he). Similarly, in reply to a question about which shirt the viewer prefers, saying 'the red one' still provides cohesion and the meaning is still understandable. For ELLs, it may be harder to maintain cohesion as readers/listeners or when producing language (speaking/writing).

COMPETENCY 2   KNOWLEDGE OF ENGLISH LANGUAGE LEARNERS

Skill 2.1   Demonstrates knowledge of the importance of providing differentiated instruction according to English Language Learners' proficiency level and diverse linguistic abilities

To meet the varied needs of ELL students, differentiating instruction becomes extremely important. With differentiated instruction, the teacher seeks to develop learning opportunities that allow students with diverse needs, abilities, and learning styles to access essential learning. This may involve creating extra opportunities for practice, reteaching, planning multiple activities, and overall flexibility in the ways in which the teacher approaches each student's needs.

It is important to note that differentiation is not the same as individualized instruction. "Every student is not learning something different; they are all learning the same thing, but in different ways. And every student does not need to be taught individually; differentiating instruction is a matter of presenting the same task in different ways and at different levels, so that all students can approach it in their own ways" (Irujo, 2004).

Students may vary in their cultural background, language, interests, learning styles/preferences, prior experiences, and learning readiness. Differentiated instruction is responsive to these differences. Important characteristics of this approach include:

- Ongoing assessment of student needs;
- Flexible grouping;
- Meaningful, authentic activities whenever possible;
- Flexibility in the learning environment; and
- Flexibility in learning activities and in the ways in which students demonstrate their learning.

This approach to instruction has the benefit of catering to students' individual needs, increasing student opportunities to perform, and developing students' personal sense of relevance and achievement. Furthermore, it leads to fewer teacher-dominated activities. Students work individually, in pairs, or in small groups on tasks and projects that cater to their different ability levels and learning styles. A number of activities can be used to help ELLs in language acquisition.

Teachers can also make use of multiple intelligence approaches to teaching the same lesson. ELLs can benefit from a variety of instructional methods that cater to their different learning preferences or styles. For example, some English Language Learners will benefit from the opportunity to learn through hands-on activities. During such activities, students learn while discussing, investigating, creating, and discovering with other students. In time, students gain background knowledge regarding the subject they are learning and start making their own decisions, leading to less teacher support and more student-centered interactions. (Cooperstein & Kocevar-Weidinger, 2004).

Skill 2.2 **Demonstrates knowledge of the many strengths, needs, interests and experiences of English Language Learners when planning instruction (i.e., instruction should be responsive to the individual needs of students, their prior educational experience, their language background, and their English proficiency levels)**

Needs Analysis
A necessary first step in planning is to conduct needs analyses which identify the proficiency level and language needs of the students involved. This helps when modifying and adjusting instruction so it will be more conducive to learning. Furthermore, attention should be given to the methodology used in class to cover the course materials. With respect to proficiency level, beginning level students require practice of material in controlled situations moving to more free expression activities. Relatively advanced learners may need to polish already developed skills and can be encouraged to involve themselves in less structured activities on their own.

Prior Knowledge, Language Literacies and Cognition/Metacognition
Moll (1988) discusses the value of the funds of knowledge that students bring to the classroom. These funds of knowledge are student's prior knowledge that can inform their acquisition of English. This knowledge regarding students' lives can be incorporated into lessons and content for course work. It also helps in choosing topics that would be of interest to the students and in engaging them in the learning process. For example, a teacher can plan a unit in which students pick an area of the city they want to learn more about. Students research their selected topics and then prepare reports or projects. Parents and family members can help students and become part of this research. Graves (1998) observes that teachers who seem to know each of their students and take an active interest in them are most successful. Teachers should also be in contact with the parents and involve them in their children's learning.

Literacy development is affected not only by the individual student's educational background but also by the linguistic background of their families. With respect to individual ESOL students, it is paramount to note that some adolescent ELLs may need to learn to read for the first time, while others are building second or third language literacy with already developed first language literacy (Peregoy & Boyle, 2000).

Literacy requires a number of cognitive and metacognitive skills that students can transfer from their first language to their second or third language. In addition to this, students literate in their first language have more funds of knowledge or prior knowledge to comprehend the content of the text. The educational background of the ELLs gives them the advantage of transferring their first language literacy skills to their second language and using their prior literacy knowledge to understand new information. With respect to writing, research has shown that students who lacked first language literacy strategies displayed a similar lack of strategies for writing in their second language. Mohan and Lo (1985) suggest that students who have not developed good strategies in their first language will not have developed strategies to transfer to their second language. Conversely, transfer of knowledge from L1 literacy helps students build literacy in their new language.

Chamot and O'Malley (1994) stated that teachers need to be aware of their students' approaches to learning and plan ways to expand the students' repertoire of learning strategies. According to Arreaga-Mayer (1998), language-sensitive content instruction based on effective and efficient learning strategies must (a) be effective for culturally and linguistically heterogeneous learning groups; (b) lead to high levels of student and student-student active engagement in learning; (c) foster higher-order cognitive processes; (d) enable students to engage in extended discourse in English; (e) be feasible to implement on a small-group or class-wide basis; (f) be socially acceptable to teachers, students, and parents; and (g) be responsive to cultural and personal diversity.

ESOL instruction is more engaging, meaningful and effective when it is based on knowledge of English Language Learners strengths, needs, interests and experiences.

Skill 2.3 **Demonstrates understanding of the importance of appropriate instructional adaptations for the many English Language Learner subgroups defined by New York State Commissioner's Regulation Part 154 (e.g., Newcomers, Developing English Language Learners, Long-term English Language Learners, Students with Inconsistent/Interrupted Formal Education [SIFE], English Language Learners with Disabilities, Former English Language Learners), as well as other subgroups of English Language Learners (e.g., heritage language speakers, gifted English Language Learners, English Language Learners with strong schooling in their home language, English Language Learners who may be multilingual, multiliterate, and multicultural)**

To guarantee that all students have the opportunity to learn and to realize their academic potential, adaptations for the groups defined above are mandated by New York State educational regulations and in some cases by federal law. See the NYSED website for details on Commissioner's Regulations Part 154: (www.nysed.gov/bilingual-ed/regulations/english-language-learnermultilingual-learner-regulations-compliance)

Because of the multitude of sub-groups defined, it is not practical in this guide to detail all possible instructional strategies. In some cases (for example, when a student has an IEP), instructional strategies will be documented for individual students to support them in meeting academic and language learning standards. For all students, however, ESOL teachers must keep in mind the importance of differentiation. If no two students are alike, then no two students learn in exactly the same way.

(See also 2.1, 2.2 and 3.5)

Skill 2.4   Demonstrates an understanding of differences between English Language Learners developing language proficiency and English Language Learners with language disorders and/or learning disabilities

Students with language disorders and/or learning disabilities are guaranteed an education under Public Law 94-142 of 1975. Learning disabilities can be any physical, emotional, cognitive or social component which severely limits learning progress. Children who fall into this category can have a range of learning challenges including emotional challenges, learning disabilities, hearing, vision or speech impairment and/or intellectually disability, etc. A key feature of the law is the requirement for an Individualized Educational Program (IEP) for any student receiving special funds for special education.

The classification of many ELLs or the "dumping" of ELLs in special education classes has been of concern to many educators. When testing English Language Learners for placement in specialized classes, you must be certain that the tests used are both reliable and valid. Reliability can be established using multiple assessment measures, objective tests, multiple raters, and clearly specified scoring criteria (Valdez-Pierce, 2003). For a test to be valid, it must first be reliable (Goh, 2004).

Learning disabilities refer to either physical, emotional, cognitive, or social components that severely limit what is considered to be "normal" functioning behavior. Children who fall into this category can be one or more of the following: emotionally challenged; hearing, vision, or speech impaired; intellectually challenged, and so on. One similarity between second language development and learning disabilities is comprehensive diagnostic testing before placement.

The typical blueprint which L2 learners follow in developing their pronunciation skills can be easily confused with a learning disability, because both categories of learners have difficulties with the same following areas: omission, substitution, distortion and addition (Lue, 2001.) These areas are the same as encountered by some L1 learners with learning disabilities.

A language disorder or learning disability is characterized by the learner experiencing difficulties in communication and speech motor skills, and typically the learner will be noticeably behind his/her classmates in language acquisition or speech skills. The following summaries outline both the similarities and differences between second language development and language disorders. Remember that an LEP learner, who has proficiency in his/her native language but struggles in the L2 environment, is not considered to have a language disorder.

Some language disorders cause the learner to:

- mispronounce phonemes (the smallest unit of a word)
- have issues with properly identifying a word in context (either verbally or nonverbally)
- have difficulty associating words and their appropriate meanings
- confuse proper grammatical structures
- have difficulty understanding advanced vocabulary
- experience difficulty following directions

All of these characteristics of language disorders are problems experienced by the L2 learner during the process of second language acquisition – the only exception being the problem with following directions. (This difficulty falls under language disorders if the learner understands directions but is not cognitively able to follow them.) During the early stages of SLA, L2 learners experience all of the characteristics that are similar to language disorders. However, this is due primarily to unfamiliarity with the structure of the L2 language, not to dysfunctions of communication or speech motor skills.

Differences: The differences between language disorders and second language learning are more apparent than their similarities. First, learners experiencing problems with speech motor skills face the following challenges:

- inability to produce certain sounds such as "r" or "l"
- voice quality issues (such as pitch or volume)
- "dysfluency" or stuttering
- difficulty creating speech that is understandable to others

The ESOL specialist bears a large responsibility for ensuring that ELLs are assessed fairly and accurately. For the long term educational and emotional well-being of ELL students, the ESOL educator may have to advocate for adequate testing, observation, and opportunities to make sure that students acquiring English are not improperly designated as having a disability.

Topics to investigate in determining whether an ELL student has a learning disability include:

- History of language delay in his/her native language;
- Difficulty in developing literacy skill in his/her native language;
- A family history of reading difficulties;
- Specific language weakness in his/her first language; and
- Relatively little progress relative to ELL peers after participating in reading interventions designed for ELL students.

Skill 2.5 **Recognizes the value and importance of encouraging active involvement of families of English language learners in the instructional program, facilitating communication between the school and families of English Language Learners and utilizing home and community resources in the ESOL program in understanding students' backgrounds (educational, linguistic, cultural)**

The ESOL teacher plays a key role in ensuring that students' families are involved in the educational program. An essential component of this is the facilitation of communication between students, families, and all teachers. Language barriers may prevent families' (and students') full participation in the learning community. By advocating for the ELL student, the ESOL instructor can ensure that the students in his or her charge are able to participate in things like the school band, science club, math club, chess club, sports teams, and all other activities students of their age and inclination participate in.

Encouraging students and their families to make full use of public resources such as the local public library, including its online resources, will help them expand their own knowledge and understanding of resources available to them. In addition, many libraries have after school, Saturday, or holiday programs to encourage constructive use of the students' time.

Museums, too, often have educational outreach programs that may be used by all citizens. Other resources such as parks and the local YMCA and YWCA (or similar organizations) offer recreational facilities to all residents.

Where possible, it is to the advantage of the ESOL instructor to be prepared to explain and if necessary suggest alternatives to the families of ELLs should educational challenges occur. Where parents are knowledgeable about their alternatives, they are better able to support their children and fully participate in the school community.

Skill 2.6 **Demonstrates knowledge of cultural, environmental, social and psychological factors within the school environment and the wider community that may affect students' English language development and academic success (e.g., age, motivation, personality, cultural contact, bias, educational variables)**

A variety of factors may have an impact on English Language Learners' academic success and language development as well as their response to the learning environment. It is important that the ESOL teacher work to create a learning environment that recognizes and responds to these factors in order to best support students' progress.

Age, gender, occupational and cultural expectations can influence a student's willingness to take risks in speaking. Because of perceived social pressure, a student just beginning to learn English in middle school may be more reluctant to try speaking in front of his/her peers than a younger child. Similarly, female students can feel 'drowned out' if teachers frequently call on boys to answer questions or reinforce stereotyped expectations about girls being quiet and well-behaved.

Beliefs and institutions have a strong emotional influence on ELLs and should always be respected. While customs should be adaptable similar to switching registers when speaking, no effort should be made to change the beliefs or institutional values of an ELL. Presenting new ideas is a part of growth, learning, and understanding. Even though the beliefs and values of different cultures often have irreconcilable differences, they should be addressed. In these instances teachers must respect alternative attitudes and adopt an "agree to disagree" attitude. Presenting new, contrasting points of view should not be avoided because new ideas can strengthen original thinking as well as change it. All presentations should be neutral, however, and no effort should be made to alter a learner's thinking. While addressing individual cultural differences, teachers should also teach tolerance of all cultures. This is especially important in a culturally diverse classroom but will serve all students well in their future interactions.

Occupation, especially in the United States, often determines one's economic status, level of prestige, and amount of power and influence. However, in other countries, regardless of how much one earns, the type of power and prestige available may largely depend on family connections or position within a particular social organization. Learner perceptions of occupations, i.e., whether a certain position is of interest or even feasible, affects second language acquisition. If education is not viewed as a realistic pathway to a career and economic security, academic success and L2 proficiency become less of a priority.

Customs play an important part in language learning because they directly affect interpersonal exchanges. What is polite in one culture might be offensive in another. For example, in the U.S., making direct eye contact is considered polite. Some cultures may view eye contact, especially with someone in a position of authority, as aggressive or rude. Teachers who are unaware of this cultural difference could offend an English Language Learner, or misjudge them, and unwittingly cause a barrier to learning. However, teachers who are familiar with this custom can make efforts not to offend the learner and can teach the difference between the two customs so that the ELL can make more informed decisions about behaviors.

Motivation
Motivation is a powerful factor in language acquisition and can take many forms. Some English Language Learners may be motivated to learn English as part of a larger goal to achieve academic and economic success. Others may be motivated to learn as part of the process of 'fitting into' or learning about a new home and culture. Still others may simply feel an intrinsic motivation to learn for learning's sake.

Researchers Gardner and Lambert (1972) have identified two types of motivation in relation to learning a second language:

- Instrumental Motivation: acquiring a second language for a specific reason, such as a job
- Integrative Motivation: acquiring a second language to fulfill a wish to communicate within a different culture

Neither type stands completely alone. Instructors recognize that motivation can be viewed as either a state or a trait. As a state, motivation is considered temporary because it fluctuates, depending on rewards and penalties. As a trait, motivation is more permanent. These factors can act as filters, causing confusion and inhibiting learning. Since language by definition is an attempt to share knowledge, the cultural, ethnic, and linguistic diversity of learners influences both their own history as well as how they approach and learn a new language. Teachers must demonstrate knowledge of the ways in which cultural and linguistic experience may impact the student's learning by taking into account many factors, including:

- the cultural background and educational sophistication of the ELL
- the exposure of the ELL to various English language variants and cultural beliefs

Self-Esteem: Learning a new language puts learners in a vulnerable frame of mind. While some learners are less inhibited about taking risks, all learners can easily be shut down if their comfort level is threatened. Using teaching techniques that reduce stress and emphasize group participation rather than techniques that focus on individuals getting the right answer reduce anxiety and encourage learners to attempt to use the new language.

Anxiety: Anxiety is inherent in second language learning. Students are required to take risks, such as speaking in front of their peers. Without a native's grasp of the language, second language learners may be unable to express their individuality, which is even more threatening and uncomfortable. However, not all anxiety is debilitative. Bailey's (1983) research on "facilitative anxiety" (anxiety that compels an individual to stay on task) is a positive factor for some learners, closely related to competitiveness.

Attitude: Attitude typically evolves from internalized feelings about oneself and one's ability to learn a language. On the other hand, one's attitude about language and the speakers of that language is largely external and influenced by the surrounding environment of classmates and family.

If non-native speakers of English experience discrimination because of their accent or cultural status, their attitude toward the value of new language learning may diminish. Schools can significantly improve the attitude towards language learning by encouraging activities between native speakers and English Language Learners. This interchange can be mutually beneficial to both groups if students learning the ELL's first language work on projects together. When native speakers get a chance to appreciate the English Language Learner's language skill in their first language, attitudes change and ELLs have an opportunity to shine. This is also one of the main ideas behind the Two-Way Dual Language Bilingual Education Model.

Acculturation is the process of becoming accustomed to the customs, language, practices, and environment of a new culture. The factors that influence this process include, but are not limited to, the learner's desire and ability to become a part of the dominant culture.

The relationship between acquiring a second language and adopting the new culture is a strong one. Schumann (1978a) has developed a model of acculturation, which asserts, "The degree to which a learner acculturates to the target language group will control the degree to which he acquires the second language." (p. 34).

According to his model, the following social elements impact the acculturation process:

- ELLs and native speakers view each other with mutual respect, have optimistic attitudes about each other.
- ELLS and native speakers both wish for the primary group to successfully assimilate.
- The length of time ELLs intend to remain in the area (e.g. short term visitors or permanent home)

These factors affect the process of acquiring English for the learners. Likewise, the absence of these factors can contribute to students not learning English and remaining outside the dominant culture. In a classroom setting, if there is no mutual respect, positive attitude, or sense of compatibility between the language learners and native speakers, successful second language acquisition for the L1 group is severely hindered. In turn, without a common language, the chances of acceptance and assimilation become significantly reduced.

It is important that the ESOL teacher try to avoid having students feel that learning English comes at the expense of their first language. This can cause negative feelings about school in general and can adversely affect second language acquisition.

Classroom and school activities that promote interactions among ELLs and native speakers encourage language growth and an exchange of cultures. With an increased ability to communicate, commonalities are discovered and friendships form. Sports, music, art, photography, and other school activities that allow ELLs to participate while they learn more language provide excellent opportunities for increasing acculturation.

Skill 2.7 Recognizes the effects of and adapts to potential cultural differences that may impact on ESOL teaching and learning (cooperation vs. competition, etc.)

In designing learning experiences, the ESOL teacher must be aware of the potential impact of cultural differences on the effectiveness of certain teaching methods. Group work, for example, has tremendous potential to create opportunities for communication and authentic language use both by ELLs and between ELLs and native speakers. This has clear benefits for student language acquisition.

Teachers, however, must be aware that cultural differences may affect how students respond to learning activities that seem engaging. Many cultures promote group loyalty and cooperation over competition and the idea of winning. Some students may be reluctant to participate in activities that they perceive could cause their peers to 'lose' or be embarrassed. Similarly, within groups some students may defer to others because of perceived status. Recognizing these potential effects will help ensure that teachers create the best possible learning situations for a diverse student body.

See also 2.6 and 2.8.

Skill 2.8   Demonstrates knowledge of ways to acknowledge and affirm various types of cultural and linguistic diversity in the ESOL classroom, the school, and the community to support instruction

ELLs often feel as if they lose a part of themselves when faced with the complexities of learning a new language and culture. To lessen these potential feelings of alienation and isolation, including elements of the ELL's culture and previous knowledge and enhance learning in the English classroom. Including culture study in the classroom may be achieved by having each student do a research project on his or her culture and report back to the class. Culture studies of this nature promote reading, writing, speaking, learning to give presentations, and creating visuals. Should there be more than one student from the same culture, pairs or small groups could be organized. Alternative types of assessment could be used to evaluate the process.

Teachers are both participants and observers in their classrooms. As such, they are in a unique position to observe what makes their students uncomfortable. By writing these observations in a teaching journal, the teacher can begin to note what activities and topics make the students in her classroom uncomfortable. If the discomfort seems to come from a lack of awareness or insensitivity to culture, it is essential to make changes to create a safe learning environment.

Another method of demonstrating sensitivity is to use appropriate teacher talk in the classroom. Wait time for student responses differ in different cultures. Students who are struggling to formulate their answers may need more time than the teacher normally gives for responding.

Different students feel comfortable with different instructional formats. These differences may be due to both cultural and individual preferences. In some cultures, cooperative group work is the norm and English Language Learners from these cultures may feel more comfortable working in collaborative groups. Students from other cultures may feel that the teacher is the only academic authority in the classroom and as such should answer questions, and their peers should not. Designing lessons that balance teacher-directed presentation, guided practice in small groups or pairs, and independent practice maximizes learning for all students.

Research has shown that a key to any successful reading program is extensive reading (Day & Bamford, 1998; Krashen, 1993). Advantages include building vocabulary, background knowledge, interest in reading, and improved comprehension. Furthermore, literacy and reading instruction are areas where multicultural sensitivity can be increased in the classroom regardless of the level of the students.

Reading materials that are culturally sensitive are necessary for the students, both native English speakers and ELLs, to have the opportunity to discuss the ways in which different cultures are alike and differ. Oral discussions of the materials will provide opportunities for comprehensible input and negotiation of meaning. Avoid materials that distort or omit certain historical events, portray stereotyping, contain loaded words, use speech that is culturally inaccurate, portray gender roles, elders and family inaccurately, and/or distort or offend a student's self-image.

Show & Tell can be another strategy for raising multicultural sensitivity. Students, particularly young ones, can bring in objects from their home culture and tell the class about their uses, where they are from, how they are made, etc.

Not all learners within the same culture learn in the same manner. Teachers need to be aware of the different ways in which students learn so that they can prepare classroom experiences and material that encompass different learning styles. By presenting content-rich, engaging and culturally diverse materials in different ways, all students are given the same opportunity to learn.

Skill 2.9   Understands the ways in which cultural, environmental, social and psychological factors may affect students' English language development (e.g., age, motivation, personality, cultural contact, bias) and applies this understanding to effectively communicate with students and their families

The same cultural, environmental, social and psychological factors that may affect a student's English language development are relevant in effective communication between the teacher, the student, and the student's family. For example, based on their own cultural experience, some parents may be reluctant to ask teachers questions if they perceive the teacher as an authority figure who should not be questioned. Others may not attend meetings with the teacher or school events if they find these situations to be intimidating because of their own limited English skills. In neither case is parents' lack of communication due to a lack of interest in their children's educational progress.

Since effective communication between the school and the home is an important factor in students' academic success, recognition of these factors is an important part of finding ways to communicate with all stakeholders in a child's education. Anticipating questions and creating a FAQ (frequently asked questions) to share with parents may help get conversations started. Similarly encouraging parents to send in questions before meetings (to avoid having to ask them directly) can also break the ice. Use of home language when possible to reach out to parents can help draw parents into the school community. Encouraging groups of parents to reach out to others in their home language is another way to connect the institution and ELL students' homes.

See also 2.6.

Skill 2.10 **Understands the ways in which social and political factors (community influence, socio-economic levels, etc.) may influence English Language Learners' language development and academic success.**

See 2.6 and 2.9

COMPETENCY 3   **ESOL INSTRUCTIONAL PLANNING, PRACTICES AND ASSESSMENT**

Skill 3.1   **Demonstrates an understanding of the theoretical bases of historical and current instructional approaches (e.g. communicative language teaching, functional- notional approach, content- based language instruction) and of different settings/models of ESOL instruction (e.g., sheltered instruction, integrated and stand alone programs) and management strategies appropriate to each in New York State classes.**

Instructional Approaches

Communicative Language Teaching or the Communicative Approach is based on the idea that interaction and communication are the primary functions of language, which is a system for expressing meaning. The application to teaching English Language Learners is that activities should involve:

- Real communication - students, teachers and others interacting and communicating
- Meaningful tasks - activities and tasks relate to real-world situations and matter to students
- Meaningful language - language is applicable to contexts and situations the learner encounters or will encounter (social, academic, workplace, subject-specific, etc.)

When engaging in the communicative approaches, activities or tasks can be adjusted to the levels and needs of the ELL. An ESOL instructor uses a variety of instructional methods to communicate with LEP students. Common techniques, suitable for all levels, are:

Contextual:
- gestures
- body language
- facial expressions
- props
- visual illustrations
- manipulatives

Linguistic Modifications (within a "natural" setting):
- standardized vocabulary
- set standard for sentence length and complexity
- reinforcement through repetition, summarization and restatement
- slower speaking pace

Teaching Vocabulary:
- use of "charades," when trying to communicate a word (acting out the word with physical actions or gestures)
- introduction of new vocabulary through familiar vocabulary
- utilization of visual props, antonyms and synonyms to communicate vocabulary

As the English Language Learner progresses, these techniques are adjusted according to individual or group needs or proficiency levels.

The goals of **The Natural Approach**, according to Krashen and Terrell (1983), were for English Language Learners to build the basic communication skills necessary for everyday communication interactions. The role of the teacher was to provide input that was understandable to the learner and/or just a little beyond their understanding so that students could learn naturally. Learners aren't expected to produce language at this early stage while teachers provide engaging activities that learners can understand, for example, activities involving games, small group work and skits. This approach is a contrast to a curriculum which requires passive listening.

Willig & Lee (1996) have specified that learners move through four developmental stages in this approach:
- **Pre-production stage** concentrates on listening comprehension and nonverbal responses from the students.
- **Early production stage** emphasizes an increasing receptive vocabulary and beginning production language.
- **Speech emergence stage** allows the student to focus on speaking in simple sentences.
- **Intermediate Fluency stage** encourages the student's ability to engage in discourse.

Total Physical Response (TPR), developed by the psychologist, James Asher, was developed as a "command-driven" instructional technique. TPR is a useful tool in the early developmental stages of second language acquisition, as well as for LEP students without any previous exposure to English, regardless of the age of the student.

Through TPR, instructors interact with students by way of commands and gestures, and the students respond physically. TPR emphasizes listening rather than speaking, and students are encouraged to speak only when they feel ready.
After numerous demonstrations by the teacher and classroom students, the entire group can act out a series of commands concerning daily events (such as going shopping, taking a bus, or preparing a simple sandwich).

The Language Experience Approach (LEA) is an instructional technique used to encourage spoken responses from LEP students after they are exposed to a variety of first-hand sensory experiences (Badia, 1966). LEA develops and improves the student's reading and writing skills by using the student's own ideas and language.

Content-based instruction (CBI) or "Sheltered Instruction" integrates L2 acquisition and the basic content areas of math, science, social studies, literature, etc. The goal in every classroom is for Limited English Proficiency (LEP) students to learn the basic content areas (math, science, social studies, etc.). To accomplish this goal, LEP students must learn an academic language which takes from five to seven years (Cummins, 1993-2003). LEP students typically encounter issues with vocabulary when being instructed in the content areas.

The most current research continues to find validity in the following:
- *Learners do not learn L2 through singular instruction in the language's rules; they learn from meaningful interaction in the language.*
- *Learners will gain proficiency in a language, only if they receive adequate input; i.e., speaking and listening start to make sense to a learner when they can build upon previous knowledge as well as understand context and cues.*
- *Although conversational fluency in L2 is a goal, speaking is not sufficient to develop the academic cognitive skills needed for learning in the basic content areas.*

The **Cognitive Academic Language Learning Approach (CALLA) (Chamot & O'Malley, 1994)** assists in the transition from an ESOL-driven language arts program to a mainstream language arts program by teaching ELLs how to handle content area material with success. CALLA helps intermediate and advanced students understand and retain content area material while they are improving their English language skills.

CALLA lessons incorporate content-area lessons based on the grade-level curriculum in science, math, social studies, etc. The student must acquire the language functions used in the content class such as describing, classifying, explaining, etc.. The learning strategy instruction will be given in critical and creative thinking skills so that ELLs develop the ability to solve problems, extrapolate, make inferences, etc.

Immersion Education Models
With these programs, instruction is initiated in the student's non-native language, using the second language as the medium of instruction for both academic content and the second language. Two of these models strive for full bilingualism: one is for language majority students and the other is for language minorities.

The major models of ESOL programs differ depending on the sources consulted. However, general consensus recognizes the following program models with different instructional methods used in the different programs:

The English as a New/Second Language (ENL/ESL) Pull-out model involves working with small groups of ELL students to target instruction to their specific needs. Students are either pulled out of regular classes or have a class specifically devoted to addressing their language needs. This time may be used in various ways to teach the ELL to communicate in social settings, engage in academic tasks, and use English in socially and culturally appropriate ways. Three well-known components of ESOL pull-out programs are:

1. **Grammar-based ESL:** teaches <u>about</u> the language, stressing its structure, functions and vocabulary through rules, drills, and error correction.
2. **Communication-based ESL:** emphasizes <u>using </u>the language in meaningful contexts. There is little stress on correctness in the early stages and more emphasis on comprehensible input to foster communication and lower anxiety when risk-taking.
3. **Content-based ESL:** attempts to develop language skills and prepare ELLs to study grade-level content material in English. Emphasis on language, but with graded introduction to content areas, vocabulary, and basic concepts.

Structured English immersion models pull ELLs out for structured instruction in English so that subject matter is comprehensible. Used with sizeable groups of ELLs who speak the same language and are in the same grade level or with diverse populations of language minority students. There is little or no L1 language support. Teachers use sheltered instructional techniques and have strong receptive skills in the students' native or heritage language.

Submersion with primary language support models are staffed with bilingual teachers or aides who support the minority students in each grade level who are ELLs. In small groups, the ELLs are tutored by reviewing the content areas in their primary language. The teachers use the L1 to support English content classes; ELLs may achieve only limited literacy in L1.

In New York State, within 10 days of enrollment, English Language Learners must be placed in an ELL program appropriate for their needs and proficiency level. The most common placement for English Language Learners is the Bilingual Education (BE) program. There are two types of programs in BE:

1. Transitional Bilingual Education Program: Home language support in content areas as students progress in English
2. Dual Language Programs: Half instruction in home language and half in English. In one-way dual language programs, the students are all ENLs with the same home language or background. In the two-way dual language program, the students are a mix of native English language speakers and ENL learners.

New York State also provides an ENL/ESL program in cases when there are many ELLs who do not speak the same home/primary language. An ESOL teacher can teach as an integrated content program or as a standalone program the ENL/ESL class.

Skill 3.2 **Applies knowledge of principles of effective literacy instruction, including data-driven instruction in essential components of reading (phonics, comprehension, etc.) and formative assessment to support literacy development in English, including identifying strategies that help English language learners utilize their spoken English to develop their reading proficiency in English.**

Formal reading instruction for English Language Learners generally incorporates the following essential components of reading:

1. Phonemic awareness
2. Phonics
3. Reading fluency
4. Vocabulary development
5. Reading Comprehension Strategies

ELL students often develop verbal skills in English before they have had an opportunity to develop reading proficiency. Using their speaking skills as a starting point for literacy development can be an effective springboard for the development of more complex reading skills. Using dialogues, plays, and other activities in which students use familiar oral language to begin developing scripts and then transitioning to more complex texts can be an accessible way of building on students existing skills to promote literacy.

Data-driven instruction and inquiry is an approach based on assessing and analyzing student data in order to adapt instructional plans to maximize student learning during the year and not just from one year to the next. With assessment of appropriate student performance tasks, teachers use data to close the gaps. The New York State Education Department expects teachers (and administrators) to assess where students are and where they need to be, to collect and analyze data to determine where students are in terms of meeting those goals, and to take action to help students throughout the year.

See 4.6, 4.8

Skill 3.3 **Demonstrates knowledge of district, state and national learning standards when planning instruction and assessment for English Language Learners**

Teachers should know, understand and work towards the achievement of district, state and national learning standards for ELLs. The national learning standards for ELLs are outlined in the Every Student Succeeds Act (ESSA) signed into law in 2015. New York State's Bilingual Common Core Initiative, launched in 2012, developed ESL standards aligned with the Common Core. Information about these standards and about bilingual education in New York state can be found on the Engage New York website, (www.engageny.org). In addition, some school districts may have additional learning standards. ESOL teachers need to incorporate district, state and national standards into instruction and assessment practices in order to support English Language Learners in become proficient in English and academically successful.

Skill 3.4 **Establishes goals for English Language Learners aligned with language development and content-area standards that offer students different pathways to success**

When working with English Language Learners, some teachers make the mistake of focusing exclusively on language development or focusing only on content-area comprehension. To maximize student learning, fluency and achievement, ESOL teachers need to align goals for learners so that as their English Language proficiency develops, so does their content-area learning and ouput. By using data-driven inquiry, formative assessment and by getting to know each learner, teachers can personalize teaching and learning so that students can meet content and language goals in multiple ways.

Skill 3.5 **Selects and designs appropriate, culturally relevant materials aligned to relevant standards (NYCCLS, New York State Bilingual Common Core Initiative–New Language Arts Progressions); scaffolds instruction to meet the needs of students with varied levels of proficiency in oracy and literacy**

It is very important that teachers choose, adapt and design instructional materials that are relevant and aligned with state learning standards. In helping students meet these standards, teachers need to be able to scaffold instruction and differentiate instruction for a range of English Language Learners.

For students with limited proficiency in English, some content can be difficult, and teachers need to implement ways to make it accessible for these students. For this purpose, teachers should encourage their students to use graphic organizers such as webs, mind-maps, Venn diagrams, and charts to help them better comprehend challenging texts. These visual tools help ELLs visualize and organize information, summarize and interpret texts and promote active learning.

The goal is that each student, through his or her own abilities, will relate to one or more techniques and excel in the learning process. While all students need to have exposure to the same curriculum, not all students need to have the curriculum taught in the same way. "Differentiation" is the term used to describe the variations of curriculum and instruction that can be provided to an entire class of students.
The following are three primary ways to differentiate:

- Content—the specifics of what is learned: This type of differentiation does not mean that whole units or concepts should be modified. However, within certain topics, specifics can be modified.
- Process—the route to learning the content: This kind of differentiation means that not everyone has to learn the content using the same method.

- Product—the results of the learning: Usually, a product is the end result or assessment of learning. For example, not all students are going to demonstrate complete learning on a quiz; likewise, not all students will demonstrate complete learning on a written paper.

Two keys to successful differentiation are:

- Knowing what is essential in the curriculum and in the learning standards. Although certain things can be modified, other things must remain intact in a specific order. Disrupting central components of a curriculum can actually damage a student's ability to learn something successfully.
- Knowing the needs of the students. While this can take quite some time to figure out, it is very important that teachers pay attention to the interests, tendencies, and abilities of their students so that they understand how each student will best learn.

Many students will need certain concepts explained in greater depth; others may pick up on those same concepts rather quickly. For this reason, teachers will want to adapt the curriculum in a way that allows students the opportunity to learn at their own pace, while keeping the class together as a community. The more creative a teacher is with the ways in which students can demonstrate mastery, the more fun the experience is for students and teachers. Furthermore, teachers reach students more successfully as they tailor lesson plans, activities, groupings, and other elements of curriculum to each student's need.

The effective teacher takes care to select appropriate activities and classroom situations in which learning is optimized. The classroom teacher should manipulate instructional activities and classroom conditions in a manner that enhances group and individual learning opportunities. For example, the classroom teacher can organize group learning activities placing students in situations in which cooperation, sharing ideas, and discussions occur. Cooperative learning activities can assist students in learning to collaborate and share personal and cultural ideas and values in a classroom learning environment.

For English Language Learners who may be struggling with language proficiency and/or with content/skill-based standards, culturally relevant materials can help motivate, inspire and connect to students' prior experience/knowledge in a meaningful way. For example, for those who may have difficulty with reading, a novel that deals with culturally familiar experiences may allow ELLs to focus on comprehension. Novels dealing with unfamiliar experiences can force a beginning ELL student to simultaneously grapple with language and subject-area skills through textual content that is new and unrelatable.

Skill 3.6   **Evaluates, selects, modifies and integrates different curricular materials (textual, non-textual, digital) in order to support English Language Learners in meeting learning goals.**

In considering suitable learning materials for the classroom, the teacher must have a thorough understanding of New York Common Core Learning Standards (NYCCLS), New York State Bilingual Common Core Initiative and New Language Arts Progressions. It is necessary that the teacher become well acquainted with the curriculum and standards for which he or she is assigned.

Keeping in mind the state requirements concerning the objectives and materials, the teacher must determine the abilities of the incoming students assigned to his or supervision. It is essential to be aware of their entry behavior—that is, their current level of achievement in the relevant areas. The next step is to take a broad overview of what students are expected to learn before they are passed on to the next grade or level of instruction. Finally, the teacher must design a course of study that will enable students to reach the necessary level of achievement, as displayed in their final assessments or exit behaviors. Textbooks and learning materials must be chosen to fit into this context.

Once students' abilities are determined, the teacher will select the learning materials for the class. In choosing materials, teachers should also keep in mind that not only do students learn at different rates, but they bring a variety of cognitive styles to the learning process. Prior experiences influence the individual's cognitive style, or method of accepting, processing, and retaining information.

Most teachers choose to use textbooks and other teaching materials which are suitable to the age and developmental level of specific student populations. They should also keep in mind the diverse background of the students and try to incorporate the different cultures in their teaching materials. Additionally, in the ESL/ENL classroom, it is recommended to use authentic texts as much as possible and to adapt them, if necessary, to the proficiency level of the students.

Aside from textual material, a wide variety of materials are available to ESOL teachers, including non-textual materials (diagrams, graphs, symbols, images, charts, etc.) and digital media. Textbook publishers and websites often provide accompanying multimedia software or links to accompany the text, as well as flow charts, graphics, and posters to help students visualize what is being taught.

One way to stay current with curricular materials is by attending online or in person workshops or conferences and by communicating regularly with other teachers in the same school. Connecting with organizations and colleagues on education websites and collaborating with others in personal learning networks helps teachers stay current, stay grounded and feel connected to educators working towards similar goals.

Educational technology can increase learning opportunities for English language students. Developing effective and adequate management and instructional strategies is crucial to integrating technology in multiple ways in the ESL/ENL classroom. Competent use of computers prevents ELLs from "academic and social marginalization" (Murray & Kouritzin, 1997, p.187). It may allow them to have more control over the direction of their learning by controlling their time, speed of learning, autonomy, choice of topics, or even their own identity (Hoven, 1992).

Technology can provide English Language learners with prompt feedback, individualized learning, and a tailored instructional sequence. It can meet specific student needs, increase their autonomy, allow for more responsibility, promote equal opportunities in a nonsexist environment, encourage student cooperation with peers, and encourage them to make decisions (Burgess & Trinidad, 1997).

Technology integration, defined by Reilly (2002), affects curriculum development and teaching practice. It is one way to move teaching from teacher- to learner-centered. To allow for greater success rates for ELLs, teachers need to integrate technology to advance student learning because technology activities, such as using the Internet or working as a team on a project, provide students with opportunities to enhance and extend the regular learning to higher levels of cognitive involvement. The effect of engaging English language students through technology can be multilayered. When technology is used as part of a model that involves students in complex authentic tasks, the results can be student-centered cooperative learning, increased teacher-student and peer interaction, and more positive attitudes toward learning, allowing greater interaction and sense of responsibility as a team.

The internet can enrich the learning process if teachers design thoughtful learning activities and assessments that incorporate it. These activities can accelerate content learning by addressing relevant information that is not solely dependent on learning English. Through experiences such as these, ELLs have the opportunities to participate in an engaging learning environment and learn at higher levels. With technology, these students can control and self-direct their learning and get immediate feedback. They no longer depend on direct teacher instruction, which often limits the student to passive listening and watching the teacher. While the direct teacher control is evidently lower in technology-based classrooms, the instruction is ever more demanding on the teacher. The teacher becomes a facilitator, rather than a "deliverer or transmitter of knowledge" (Padrón & Waxman, 1996, p. 348). Teachers scaffold their students' learning experiences to build high-quality instruction.

The following are some activities using technology that are intended to support learner knowledge construction:

1. Collaborating with others around the world
2. Utilizing educational applications of the internet
3. Creating multimedia projects (Hartley & Bendixen, 2001)

When students are engaged in activities like these, they are constructing their own knowledge, with the teacher as the facilitator of the process. It is essential that teachers encourage students to be thoughtful and reflective about their technology use. It is also ideal if teachers who use technology extensively in the classroom infuse digital and media literacy throughout content and language based learning so that students apply critical thinking skills to digital media texts and textual interactions.

Incorporating technology effectively into a fully content- and skill-based curriculum requires a good understanding of lesson objectives and how those objectives can be met using the technology. While teachers should definitely consider technological integration as an important aspect of their work in any subject and at any grade level, teachers should not include technology simply for the sake of technology. The best approach, considering that all subjects can potentially be enhanced with technology, is for the teacher to consider a variety of lessons and units and decide which focus areas can be enhanced with technological tools.

It is important to remember that as with all other learning, technological learning must be developmentally appropriate. Concerns about excessive screen time and the importance of face-to-face interaction, especially with young students, are important factors to consider.

Skill 3.7   Ensures classroom communication practices (positive interactions, clear instructions, varied content presentation, etc.) that facilitate English Language Learners' understanding and language learning

In order to maximize learning, the learning environment needs to be positive, safe and encouraging of risk-taking, mistakes and and practice. Teachers should demonstrate knowledge of techniques that create a positive learning environment for all students. The NYSED's Blueprint for Success outlines the need for ESOL teachers to provide a safe and inclusive learning environment for all students incorporating culturally and linguistically appropriate materials and "language focused scaffolds." (http://www.nysed.gov/common/nysed/files/programs/bilingual-ed/nysblueprintforellsuccess.2016.pdf)

In addition, in order to make content accessible, teachers need to determine the appropriate level of language to use for instruction for the given ELL population. Additionally, teachers should (Loughlin & Haynes, 1999):

- Simplify the language of instruction, not the content being taught.
- Eliminate nonessential information and present materials in a clear, concise, and comprehensible manner.
- Teach the material in multiple ways, through oral, visual, auditory, and kinesthetic learning modalities.
- Pre -teach content area vocabulary and concepts, using realia, picture files, and hands-on activities.
- Check for comprehension during instruction and structure speaking and writing opportunities for students.

- Use or create materials that simplify the language of abstract concepts by retelling content information in easier English. Depending on the proficiency level of the students, teachers should use simple sentence structure and high frequency verbs.
- Select materials that help students build connections and associations in order to access background knowledge or previously taught information. This can be accomplished through teacher-prepared outlines and study guides.
- Present students with written as well as aural messages. Outline what you are saying on the chalkboard.
- Allow students' use of native language for English language and concept development.
- Model think-alouds to increase student comprehension. *Think-alouds* are oral demonstrations of the teacher's own cognitive processes or the strategies they use to comprehend a text. Students then try to incorporate these strategies to help themselves in the learning process. Teachers explicitly teach these strategies until the learners are able to use them independently.

Skill 3.8   Promotes English Language Learners' learning engagement through meaningful learning experiences that are challenging, set high expectations and encourage students to take responsibility for their learning; fosters a respectful, safe, student-centered learning environment that encourages participation, cooperation and learning

With high expectations, a positive classroom environment, solid structures in place for learning and clear communication, English Language Learners are more likely to succeed academically and to become more proficient in English. Second language acquisition theorists and theories about learning in general, argue that meaningful interaction is a crucial element in student learning. Authentic tasks, relevant instructional materials (including realia), communication and interaction opportunities with peers, teachers and the community outside the school help motivate students to learn and to care about what they are learning.

This does not mean classroom activities and tasks should be easy; in fact teachers should strive to challenge students both with the activities themselves and the expectations they have for success. Students will be inspired both by the expectations and the belief that teachers have that they can meet them. The choices teachers make about the types of instructional texts to use and the reading, writing, speaking and listening activities around those texts are very important. Texts should be engaging, meaningful, relevant and full of big ideas and rich supporting details and content. There should be plenty of classroom talk and discussion to tease out the ideas, to practice conversations about texts as well as the academic language used to discuss them and frequent/daily writing activities that help learners develop their knowledge base and their language skills.

Classroom organization has a significant influence on the language learning process. The second language classroom is a student-centered classroom where students work individually or in small groups on assigned tasks and projects. Classroom organization that focuses on learner-centered instruction provides students with greater opportunities to perform productively in the target language, as well as a sense of achievement and personal success.

In general, pair and group work are considered the most effective and meaningful classroom organization techniques. Classroom-centered research has demonstrated that pair and group work give students a great deal of opportunity to engage in meaningful communication, and they also perform as well with respect to grammatical accuracy as when the teacher is leading the discussion.

Pair work
Pair work helps students engage in meaningful conversations that lead to the use of language to exchange ideas and information with a fellow student. To promote effective pair work, students should engage in tasks that require exchange of information in order to be successfully completed. Activities like "Information Gap" require students to negotiate information in order to complete the task.

Group work
Group work is considered to generate meaningful discussions (negotiation of meaning) that lead to a greater meaningful use of the target language, which facilitates learning. ELLs participating in interactive discussion tasks use a wide range of language as opposed to ELLs in larger groups discussing the same question, with the teacher leading the discussion. Working in larger groups can make ELL students' responses shorter or less complex. In contrast, the smaller group provides a relaxed atmosphere which benefits students' language production. A productive group would be two to five students performing "task-based consensus activities".

Additionally, some students avoid speaking in front of the whole class, but those same students can be more comfortable interacting in small groups. Therefore, group work utilizes class time effectively and also produces more complex speech, encouraging students to take risks and produce spontaneous speech. This process leads to cooperative learning where students work together to complete the task at hand. Within a group, students are assigned roles (*leader, time manager, speaker, etc.*) to make sure all the members of the group participate.

Whole class cooperative learning
Just as individuals contribute in a group, different groups can also contribute to the creation of whole-class cooperative activities. Different groups produce work that brings forward diverse ideas. If the teacher assigns student groups different tasks or roles, they can effectively collaborate by sharing responsibilities to complete whole-class tasks. This approach engages different groups within a classroom to collectively work towards completion of a project. An example would be jigsaw reading where each group is assigned one reading or part of a reading which further requires them to work with other groups to combine their respective parts to make sense of the whole reading.

An important part of the learning process for all learners is encouraging students to be reflective about their strengths, challenges and strategies for success. When students take responsibility for their own learning, they will be able to do what teachers do; set goals, assess their progress, analyze their needs and make action plans to improve their learning and proficiency. In order for ELLs to do this, they need to feel comfortable asking questions, and admitting when they don't understand or need input to be repeated. A respectful, safe, cooperative classroom environment is crucial in helping students improve academic, communicative, and metacognitive skills.

Skill 3.9   Demonstrates knowledge of different types of assessments (e.g., norm- and criterion-referenced, standardized, formative, summative) and important concepts used in evaluating the usefulness, purpose and appropriateness of an assessment (e.g. reliability, validity, practicality) and applies strategies for integrating assessment with ESOL instruction

Assessment is one of the most important parts of an ESOL teacher's job for many reasons. First, assessment helps teachers personalize and differentiate learning opportunities for students. Second, assessment can inform and transform instruction. Third, assessment can help students take more responsibility for their learning by providing them with opportunities to reflect on goals and progress.

In addition to standard tests, informal assessment is an effective way to test students' progress regularly. This helps teachers focus on students' problem areas, adapt instruction, and ensure learning. Typical classroom activities are used to measure progress with respect to curricular goals and objectives. There are three commonly used informal methods: portfolio assessment, conferencing/interviews/observation and performance-based assessment.

Portfolio Assessments
Portfolios are a collection of the student's work over a period of time (report cards, creative writing, and drawing, and so on) that also function as an assessment tool. They indicate a range of competencies and skills and are representative of instructional goals and academic growth.

Portfolio assessments help teachers maintain a record of their students' work for the entire school year. This makes it possible for both teachers and students to view students' progress throughout the year. Portfolios include information, sample work, and evaluations that serve as students' progress records. (See 4.15)

Digital portfolios are particularly useful because they can easily accommodate just about any type of student work and are 'portable', meaning that students can continue to build their portfolios throughout their education.

Conferencing/Interviews/Observation

Conferencing allows the instructor to evaluate a student's progress or decline. Students also learn techniques for self-evaluation.

Teacher Observation is an essential assessment tool in which the instructor observes the student behavior during an activity alone or within a group. Before the observation occurs, the instructor may want to create a scale or rubric to record and measure achievement and desired outcomes.

Documentation shares similarities with teacher observations. However, documentation transpires over a longer period of time than isolated observations.

Performance-Based Assessment Activities

This type of assessment is based on the tasks and activities done in the classroom. Some of the activities are oral reports, presentations, demonstrations, and written assignments. Both process (e.g., several drafts of a writing sample) as well as product (e.g., research paper) can become a part of this assessment. This approach helps to monitor the student's growth over a period of time and get a real sense of their improvement. Scoring rubrics and observation checklists can be utilized to evaluate the student's ability and progress. It is important to have clear and fair evaluation criteria from the beginning. Some performance-based activity examples are:

Content-based interviews, which allow teachers to evaluate the language the students are using and/or an ELL's ability to provide content information when asked questions—both of which have implications for further instructional planning.

General interviews, which allow instructors to evaluate the student's level of English proficiency, as well as to identify potential problem areas which may require correctional strategies.

Student journals, which are beneficial for students as written records and as tools used to promote and develop an inner dialogue (metacognition).

Story or text retelling, which can be used as a form assessment so that when students respond orally, they can be assessed on how well they describe events in the story or text as well as on their response to the story and their language proficiency.

Experiments and/or demonstrations, which can be used to assess English Language Learners' understanding of a concept, and explanation of a method or process as well as their language proficiency.

Self-assessments, when combined with goal-setting, can be an effective way for students to help students take an active role in their learning. Teachers need to provide guidance as well as the criteria related to success, especially at the beginning of any process of self-assessment.

Factors That May Affect Assessment Results

Certain factors may affect the assessment of ELLs who are not familiar with assessment in the U.S. classroom. Among these is unfamiliarity with standard testing techniques. Students may become disconcerted when they are not allowed to ask questions of the teacher, are restricted by time constraints, or are permitted to work only on certain sections of the test at a time.

Other students may also be uncomfortable when ELLs are allowed specific accommodation during the test session. Accommodations allowed by the test publisher or those prescribed by the state need to be introduced in the regular classroom so that ELLs and other students are familiar with them before the testing session begins.

The constructs of reliability and validity are crucial in assessing ELLs because of the high stakes involved in testing in today's schools. Decisions about schools, teachers, and students are based on these tests. A reliable assessment test for ELLs will have the following three attributes: validity, reliability, and practicality.

Validity: An assessment test can only be considered "valid" if it measures what it asserts to measure. If an ELL assessment test claims to measure oral proficiency, then the test should include a section where instructors ask the ELL learner to pronounce certain words, listen to the instructor's pronunciation, and determine if it is correct and/or ask the learner to respond directly to the instructor's questions.

According to Díaz-Rico & Weed (1995), "Empirical validity is a measure of how effectively a test relates to some other known measure." There are different types of validity: predictive and concurrent (Díaz-Rico & Weed, 1995). "Predictive" empirical validity is concerned with the possible outcomes of test performance, while, "concurrent" empirical validity is connected with another variable for measurement. For example, if a learner shows a high amount of English speech proficiency in class, then the instructor would have the expectation that the learner would perform well during an oral proficiency exam.

Reliability: An assessment test can only be considered "reliable" if similar scores result when the test is taken a second time. Factors such as anxiety, hunger, tiredness, and uncomfortable environmental conditions should not cause a huge fluctuation in the learner's score. Typically, if a learner earns a score of 90% on a test that was created by the instructor, then averages predict that the learner probably scored 45% on one half of the test and 45% on the other half, regardless of the structure of the test items. If this prediction holds true, the test has high reliability.

Practicality: A test that proves to be both valid and reliable may unfortunately prove to be cost- or time-prohibitive. The ideal assessment test would be one that is easy to administer, easy to grade, and includes testing items closely similar to what the learners have experienced in class. However, when learners encounter test items such as writing journals, practicality becomes an issue. A writing journal, although an excellent method for learners to explore their critical literacy skills as well as track language achievement progress, can be difficult to grade due to the subjective content, and it may not act as a fair representation of what the learners have encountered in class.

Skill 3.10 **Recognizes the importance of using and embedding multiple forms of assessment in instruction to measure and document English Language Learners' progress and applies knowledge of how to analyze formal and informal methods of assessing specific dimensions of language proficiency to adjust or plan instruction**

Reading and Writing Assessments

Assessing specific dimensions of English Language proficiency is complex. For testing the reading abilities of English Language Learners, Hughes (1989) presents a framework which includes content (operations, types of text, addresses, and topics) and criteria levels of performance.

Content

Operations: Operations include different levels of analysis that require attention. These comprise the macro-skills that cover the objectives of the course and the needs of the students and include:

- identifying stages of an argument
- identifying examples in support of an argument
- scanning text to locate specific information
- skimming text to obtain the gist

These also include micro-skills such as:

- using content to guess meaning of unfamiliar words
- identifying referents of pronouns, etc.
- recognizing indicators in discourse, especially for the introduction, development, transition, and conclusion of ideas

There should be a balance of the macro and micro skills tested which reflects the relationship between the two levels of skill.

Types of text: The designer of the test should identify the type of text used for the test, such as textbook, novel, magazine, newspaper, academic journal, letter, poem, etc. Additionally, the use of authentic texts depends in part on what the test is intended to measure. It is possible to use authentic text at lower levels of abilities.

Addresses and Topics: This element is related to test types and specifies the audience of a particular type of text. The range of topics can be mentioned in general terms.

Setting criteria levels of performance: In a norm-referenced approach to testing, student performance is evaluated by comparison with others. In criterion-referenced approach, it is specified what the candidate should know to achieve a specific level.

However, it can be difficult with reading to provide interpretation of scores (e.g., what does a student know if s/he gets 60 or 70 %?). It would be best to use the test task itself to define the level (Hughes, 1989). For example, in order to pass, the student should be able to score a particular number of items correct (say 80 per cent). Additionally, while scoring, errors of grammar, spelling or punctuation should not be penalized if the student is able to successfully complete the task.

Setting the tasks
Selecting the texts:

- Keep the content and the criteria level in mind when selecting a text.
- Choose text of appropriate length. For example, scanning may require a longer passage (approx. 2000 words) as opposed to detailed reading.
- To obtain reliability, include as many passages as possible in order to give candidates ample chances to show performance level.
- Choose a text of interest to the students.
- Texts should be avoided that contain information that is part of the students' general knowledge, which would enable them to answer questions without reading the passage.

Writing items
The purpose of the test items should be to elicit reliable performance and reliable scoring. The items should be within the capabilities of the students and should make minimal demands on their writing skills. Those items should be avoided for which the correct response can be found without understanding the text. Also, paragraph numbers and line numbers should be added to the text if items need to make reference to them. It is very important to get the opinion of colleagues on the text and the test items.

Possible Techniques: The items should interfere as little as possible with the reading itself and avoid asking students to write answers in response to the reading passage. Some of the methods used are:

- Multiple choice: Students are provided with choices from which they select the correct answer. True/False questions are also a variety of multiple choice.
- Unique answer: In this task type, there is only one possible correct answer. This might be a single word or number, or something a little longer. The test item may be a question, however, this form is not recommended for extensive use.
- Short answer/Guided short answer: Short answer items can be used when unique answer items are not possible. However, it may again be a problem that students are not able to express themselves through writing. Guided short answer items provide partial information to students so that they have only to complete sentences already given to them. For example: "Many universities in Europe used to insist that their students speak and write only _____. Now many of them accept _____ as an alternative, but not a _____ of the two." Hughes (1989)

- Summary cloze: In this technique, a reading passage is summarized and gaps are left in the summary for students to complete. Similar to guided answers, this is a more reliable way of testing reading comprehension than unique answer items.
- Information transfer: Another way of limiting the demands on students' writing ability is to ask them to perform successful completion of a reading task, transferring simple information in different ways, such as a table, following a route on a map, labeling a picture, or numbering a series of events.

In addition, there are a multitude of tests for evaluating, assessing, and placing ELLs in the appropriate programs. Each test can evaluate a narrow range of language skills (such as discrete tests designed to measure grammar sub-skills or vocabulary).

A language test should be chosen on the basis of the information it gives, the appropriateness of the instrument for the purpose, and the soundness of the test content. Language has over two hundred dimensions which can be evaluated, and yet most tests assess fewer than twelve of them. Therefore, all language testing should be done cautiously; backed up by teacher observations, oral interviews, and family life variables; and grounded in school records.

Assessment should be used to plan and adjust instruction for whole classes, small groups and individual learners. Using a combination of formal and informal assessments and data-driven inquiry to focus instruction and to help English Language Learners achieve English language proficiency and academic success.

Additionally, when designing and analyzing writing assessments, ESOL teachers should be aware of the following potential goals.

1. Set writing tasks that are properly representative of the type of tasks that we should expect the students to be able to perform.
2. The tasks should elicit samples of writing which truly represent the student's ability.
3. Writing samples should be scored reliably. (Hughes (1989))

A well-structured writing test does the following:

Specifies all appropriate tasks and selects a sample
When preparing the test, it is essential that the tasks represent what we expect the students to be able to perform on the test. This should be identified before we start creating the test.

Focuses on writing
Writing tests for ELLs should not set tasks that evaluate students' intelligence, general knowledge, or good support for their opinions. Additionally, we should not make the instructions so difficult or long that the students have problems comprehending them.

Presents well-defined tasks
When responding to a task, students should know what is required of them and should not stray from the topic. However, teachers should be careful not to provide too much information in the instruction which could help students perform the task. For example, complete sentences should be avoided which could be used in the composition.

Presents tasks that can be scored reliably:

1. **Holistic scoring**: In this type of scoring, a single score is given to the writing piece on the basis of an overall impression. This helps to score quickly and therefore one piece of writing can be scored more than once to ensure reliability. However, this scoring system should be appropriate to the level of the candidates and the purpose of the test.
2. **Analytic methods of scoring**: This method of scoring requires a separate score for each of a number of subskills. The number varies according to the purpose of the test and may include grammar, vocabulary, mechanics, fluency (style of communication), and form (organization). This kind of scoring helps assess and diagnose all subskills as well as make the test reliable because each test is given a number of scores (one for each subskill). However, the scoring takes longer and the division into subskills might divert the assessment from the overall effort of the writing.

The choice of the type of scoring depends on the purpose of the test, but it is important that the scorers should be trained in using these scales. Additionally, each writing sample of the student should be scored independently by two or more scorers and should be recorded on separate sheets. A third member of the test team should search for any discrepancies in the scores given to the same piece of writing.

In addition to listening and speaking assessments (see 4.4 and 4.5), which must also consider similar factors to the reading and writing assessments (see 3.10), there are language placement, language proficiency and language achievement tests, which will also be used to adapt or plan instruction.

Language Placement Tests
A language placement test is designed to place a student within a specific program. The school district may design its own instrument or use a standardized test. For example, the New York State Identification Test for English Language Learners (NYSITELL) assesses the English level of new students to determine ELL status and the level of support within the ELL program.

Language proficiency tests
These tests measure how well students have met certain standards in a particular language. The standards have been predetermined and are unrelated to any course of study, curriculum, or program. These tests are frequently used to enter or exit a particular program. For example, the New York State English as a Second Language Achievement Test is an annual assessment for all ELLs to assess English proficiency, and helps determine when a student can exit the ELL program (with continued support).

Language achievement tests

These tests relate directly to a specific curriculum or course of study. The tests include language sub-skills, reading comprehension, parts of speech, and other mechanical parts of the language such as spelling, punctuation, and paragraphing. Examples of language achievement tests are unit exams and final exams.

Diagnostic language tests

These tests are designed to identify individual students' strengths and weaknesses in language in general. They are generally administered by speech therapists or psychologists in clinical settings when specific language learning problems are present.

Formative Assessment Tools

In addition, classroom teachers can use portfolios, conferencing, interviews, observation and documentation, student self-assessment and journaling, story or text retelling, experiments and/or demonstrations to assess language proficiency and adapt instruction. (See 3.9.)

Skill 3.11 Applies methods of facilitating communication between all stakeholders (school, families, community members, teachers, English Language Learners) about assessment results, progress and instructional practice

New York State Department of Education requires schools to inform parents when children have been identified as English Language Learners and requires the school to provide an orientation session to parents informing them of state standards, school expectations, tests, and program goals and requirements. In addition, parents should be provided with ongoing information about their child's language progress and development including the opportunity to attend a meeting with teachers and/or other school staff.

Often in schools, parents, grandparents, and other people involved in children's lives, want to take a more active role in the educational process. It is important to provide opportunities for the public to come into the school and participate in activities designed to encourage their participation in the schooling of their children. During these programs, it is important to share information about the methodologies and strategies being implemented to support students. In this way, the public can begin to understand the methodology and programs used in ESOL instruction.

Taking the time to educate parents and other family members not only helps to enhance understanding and open communication, it can also provide more support for students than the school alone would ever be able to provide.

Some strategies for educating parents and family members include:

- open house style events
- parent workshops on various topics

- newsletter pieces or paragraphs
- individual parent meetings
- inviting parents to observe lessons
- information shared during social times where parents are invited into the school

Communicating general information about English and appropriate English language instruction is important. It is just as important to share specific information about students with parents, other school personnel, and the community. Once the teacher has gathered sufficient information on the students, s/he must find appropriate methods to share this information with those who need the data. Again, depending on the audience, the amount and type of information shared may vary. Some ways to share information with parents/guardians include:

- individual parent meetings
- small group meetings
- regular parent updates through phone calls, email, or other messaging tools
- charts and graphs of progress sent home
- class blogs or portals on learning management systems

When teachers communicate clearly, consistently and meaningfully with parents and families, colleagues, administrators and the English Language Learners themselves, the stakeholders are more likely to work together towards the common goal of helping learners achieve communication, academic and social/emotional success. Communicating about assessment methods and results is important, but so is communicating about instructional practice so that stakeholders understand the goals and the strategies for meeting goals. Stakeholders can then more effectively help develop student strengths and meet student needs.

Skill 3.12   **Understands issues (past educational experience, bias, norm groups, etc.) that can affect the validity of assessments of English Language Learners; national, state, and local requirements for determining English Language Learners placement and progress in the ESOL program (e.g., New York State Commissioner's Regulation Part 154)**

The New York State Department of Education, Bilingual Education & English as a New Language program office contains links to a clearly articulated Blueprint for Success (for ELLs) and Regulations and Compliance documents (for districts and schools) on their website (http://www.nysed.gov/bilingual-ed) in addition to resources for educators and parents.

It is essential for teachers to understand regulations and requirements related to instruction, assessment and reporting and to understand the issues that may affect student achievement on national, state and school tests.

Instructors of LEP students need to be aware of the less obvious cultural and linguistic bias in tests, such as students who are unfamiliar with the test-taking techniques of multiple-choice questions and/or bubble answer sheets.

Cultural bias

Cultural bias concerns the way knowledge acquired from participating in and sharing certain cultural values and experiences shapes opinions and attitudes. Asking questions about things like birthdays or holiday celebrations may presume learners have knowledge of experiences they have not shared. Many ELLs come from backgrounds and cultures with different traditions.

Attitudinal bias

This type of bias refers to the negative attitude of the examiner towards a certain language, dialect, or culture. Just as high expectations from instructors can lead to high results in classroom performance (the Pygmalion Effect), when a negative attitude is evident in the assessor, teacher or school culture, ELLs may demonstrate lower scores on assessments of progress.

Test bias or norming bias

This term refers to the exclusion during development of the testing tool of subgroups who will be assessed by a standardized test. Exclusion need not be deliberate for this to occur. As an example of norm bias, a test may include questions that assume background knowledge that large numbers of test-takes do not share (e.g., ELL students who are not familiar with certain terms or references not connected to the skills or knowledge being assessed).

Translation bias

When the test is literally translated from its original language to the language being learned by interpreters or other means, the "essence" of the test may be lost because it is difficult to translate cultural concepts.

Anxiety

Test anxiety for an ELL may go well beyond what is considered "normal" anxiety for a native English speaker. ELLs are potentially at a much greater disadvantage. Not only is there "anxiety" about studying for a test, the test format itself could be unfamiliar, depending on the ELLs' culture and previous test-taking experience. Multiple choice questions and "cloze" or fill-in-the-blanks, can be intimidating, and such formats may not be true indicators of the ELLs' actual level of proficiency (Díaz-Rico & Weed, 1995). A potential "workaround" to reduce the ELLs' anxiety would be to administer practice tests to allow the ELL to develop a comfort level.

Time Limitations

Time may create issues for ELLs. In the U.S., it is customary for the instructor to assign a class period to complete an exam, or for language learners to take statewide school achievement tests in a timed, non-negotiable fashion. ELLs may need additional time, depending on their comfort level and experience.

Instructor/Learner Rapport
If the ELL does not share a comfortable relationship with the instructor, and/or there are significant language barriers between them, the ELL may not be forthcoming about any questions or clarification about the test. Without the ability or comfort level to address these issues, the ELL's success could be compromised before the test begins. Furthermore, nuances of the English language, idiomatic phrasing, and confusing instructions can also negatively impact the ELL's test performance.

Skill 3.13   Demonstrates knowledge of acceptable assessment accommodations for current and former English Language Learners defined by NYSED, as well as NY State interventions (RTI and AIS)

See 5.10 and the New York State Department of Education, Bilingual Education website for details. (http://www.nysed.gov/bilingual-ed)

Skill 3.14   Understands federal accountability rules for English Language Learners and potential impacts on instruction

The Every Student Succeeds Act (ESSA, 2015) sets out federal accountability rules for states, districts and schools with regard to English Language Learners on its website (http://www.ed.gov/essa). You can also read a thorough explanation of federal and state provisions of the act related to English Language Learners on the National Association of State Boards of Education website: (http://www.nasbe.org/wp-content/uploads/Parsi_ELLESSA-Final-3.pdf)

COMPETENCY 4   INSTRUCTING ENGLISH LANGUAGE LEARNERS IN ENGLISH LANGUAGE ARTS

Skill 4.1   Applies understanding of NYCCLS and New York State Bilingual Common Core Initiative–New Language Arts Progressions to language and literacy instruction for English Language Learners at varying levels of proficiency

New York State's Engage NY site contains dozens of resources to help teachers both understand the theoretical foundations of and implement the New York State Bilingual Common Core Initiative–New Language Arts Progressions. The site contains PDFs outlining the standards: (https://www.engageny.org/resource/new-york-state-bilingual-common-core-initiative).

Each progression outlines the main academic and linguistic demands for each common core standard as well as performance indicators (with scaffolds) for how students at different ELL levels can meet the standards in reading, writing, listening and speaking.

It is essential that ESOL teachers understand the Common Core and New Language Arts Progressions and the performance indicators used to assess them. These standards and progressions should be used to plan and guide both assessment and instruction of language and literacy. The standards are intended to help students maximize language proficiency and content-area learning and to help teachers design instruction that engages students in meaningful activities to make maximum learning progress.

Skill 4.2   Demonstrates knowledge of the transferability of first- language literacy skills into English.

With respect to individual ESOL students, it is paramount to note that some ELLs are building second or third language literacy with already developed first language literacy (Peregoy & Boyle, 2000). Literacy requires a number of cognitive and metacognitive skills that students can transfer from their first language to their second or third language.

In addition to this, students literate in their first language have more funds of knowledge or prior knowledge to comprehend the content of the text. The educational background of the ELLs gives them the advantage of transferring their first language literacy skills to their second language and using their prior literacy knowledge to understand the new information. With respect to writing, research has shown that students who lacked first language literacy strategies displayed a similar lack of strategies for writing in their second language. Mohan and Lo (1985) suggest that students who have not developed proficient strategies in their first language will not have developed strategies to transfer to their second language. Conversely, transfer of knowledge from L1 literacy helps students develop essential English language writing skills.

Furthermore, family literacy of the English language learners also has an impact on their literacy development. Educational level of the parents has a great influence on literacy development. In families where reading for pleasure is the norm, for example, students are more likely to develop similar reading habits in English. Parents who read books to children from an early age and have books, newspapers, magazines, and other reading materials available at home, facilitate their children's literacy development. These families spend time reading together and encourage critical thinking and higher order skills in their children. Parents with positive attitudes towards education may be more likely to have high academic expectations for their children and feel comfortable getting involved in their education. These positive attributes help students develop skills that lay the foundation for success in school.

(See Skill 9.2 for more details on reading transferability)

Skill 4.3   Recognizes the importance and interdependence of integrating the five skills (reading, writing, listening, speaking and viewing) to promote language development; uses research-based methods to promote communicative competence in the English Language Arts

Though there are times in which it may be necessary to teach specific skills in isolation (e.g., when a student continues to struggle with a particular grammatical structure in his/her writing), in general it is far better to approach language acquisition holistically, by integrating reading, writing, speaking, listening, and viewing. This approach encourages natural interactions with language and exposes ELLs to authentic language. Chamot and O'Malley (1994) demonstrate that content and language learning can be integrated with their Cognitive Academic Language Learning Approach (CALLA).

Other models that integrate the learning of content with language development are adjunct, sheltered, and theme-based (Scarcella and Oxford, 1992). Theme-based instruction centers around the use of the five core skills of of language to communicate about a central theme or topic. Students may, for example, participate in writing activities, plays, and speeches to both demonstrate their learning while also building language skills. In the sheltered model ELLs learn essential content from different subject areas using simplified language or texts and other methods of scaffolding to build understanding. In The Adjunct Model, language and content teachers carefully coordinate instruction but teach separately until the English Language Learner is ready to join a classroom without language support.

Task-based instruction, another model for integrating the five communicative skills of language arts, involves increasingly complex learning tasks that require students to use language in authentic cooperative tasks such as projects, plays, or writing. These cooperative tasks simultaneously reinforce and build on ELLs' language skills. For example, in creating a book talk with a partner, students read, speak with partners, write a script, speak and listen.

The integrated approach offers many benefits. It is often more engaging for students, offers opportunities for ELLs to communicate with their peers, and shows English as a 'living' language (as opposed to learning skills in isolation). It allows teachers to evaluate student progress towards content and language standards, and integration of skills is beneficial for all English language learners, regardless of their proficiency level (Genesee et. al., 2006).

The integration of the five skills provides an effective context for writing so that the use of one leads naturally to the use of another, as in real life. In this way, the learners will see how writing relates to certain communicative needs just as the other skills do. For example, students need to participate in classroom conversations by articulating their opinions, sharing their observations, making comparisons, etc., through speaking and writing. They need to listen to the topic, take notes, discuss with their classmates, and read about the topic which requires the integration of all four skills.

English Language Learners need to engage in real-life communicative situations, so classroom activities should be organized in a way to make them use all five skills. Students should not only speak with the teacher but also with other students. As an example, students can listen to peers and try to comprehend what each speaker is saying. The listener can then react by writing down for a reader her/his version of the information s/he has just heard. This sequence of activities helps students connect listening, speaking, reading, and writing. There is thus very little opportunity for the student to translate his/her idea from his/her native language into English.

Prewriting techniques can give students opportunities to use reading, writing, listening and speaking to help them explore and get started with their ideas on a given topic or to develop a topic for a writing activity based on communicative classroom activities.

Brainstorming
- Brainstorming lets students work together in the classroom in small groups to say as much as they can about a topic. This process helps them generate ideas to use for their individual brainstorming on paper. This activity involves the use of both speaking and listening skills to produce effective writing.

Guided Discussion
- Another way to get students to talk about a topic or to focus on specific aspects of a topic is to provide guidelines for group or whole class discussion. This technique has the advantage of helping the students beforehand with the vocabulary and sentence forms that they might need in their discussion, making use of all the four skills to guide students in their writing process.

Other activities that can incorporate all five skills students include:
- interviews
- creating movies, podcasts, posters
- skits
- dictation

- note-taking
- story-telling

Skill 4.4   Applies knowledge of research- and evidence-based methods and resources for supporting and scaffolding English Language Learners' achievement of relevant learning standards related to English listening skills (e.g., integrate and evaluate information presented in diverse media and formats; evaluate a speaker's point of view, reasoning, and use of evidence)

Listening is now not considered a 'passive' skill, but a dynamic process that can make a lot of demands on language learners. Keeping in mind the complex nature of processing spoken language, a combination of bottom-up and top-down approaches have been recommended. The bottom-up processing of listening refers to analysis of the language by the listener to find out the intended meaning of the message.

On the other hand, the top-down processing relies on the listener's bank of prior knowledge and global expectations. Prior knowledge allows the learners to make predictions about the incoming message on the basis of the context in which the interaction is taking place. Top-down processing involves prediction and inference on the basis of the listener's background knowledge regarding the participants in the situation, their roles and purposes, the typical procedures adopted by the participants of the interaction, and their consequences.

Educational psychologists posit that verbal learning becomes easier when information can be chunked into meaningful patterns and then related to existing meaning structures - *schemata*. Carrell and Eisterhold (1983) discovered that background knowledge in the listener's mind is of two types: content schemata and formal schemata. Content schemata include familiarity with the topic, cultural knowledge, and previous experience with a field. Formal schemata deals with people's knowledge of discourse forms: text types, rhetorical conventions, and the structural organization of prose. Both content and formal schemata can help listeners in comprehension.

This understanding indicates that English language learners should be made familiar with the topic under discussion and the structure and type of text under consideration in order to tap into students' schemata and previous global experiences. This front-loading of connections would aid the students in listening comprehension and help them develop skills to become proficient listeners.

Usually when we listen to something, we have certain expectations and a purpose for listening. We have some idea about the content, formality level, etc. in the discourse that we are about to hear. Some ideas are based on "script competence", which is the knowledge the listeners possess in advance about the context or the subject matter of the discourse. These expectations are often linked to the purpose for listening. People listen to specific information or details depending on the purpose or the task at hand (enjoyment, knowledge, persuasion, social or expression).

Listening for gist is to get the general idea or meaning. This means ignoring the details and following the overall topic even if you do not understand every word – for example, listening to the news every day to get a general idea of what is happening in the world. Conversely, someone could understand all the words that form a news story, but without context about the situation being reported, s/he could easily not understand what was being said. Additionally, if a person listens only for enjoyment or entertainment (like listening to a conversation), he or she will only focus on the overall message.

On the other hand, *listening for details* means to get the specific facts. The focus is to selectively extract information to suit one's purpose. For example, if we want to know the answer to a question and expect to hear the appropriate response, this makes us listen for key phrases or words. When we ask a question like, "Where are you going?", we listen for the particular expression of place. Additionally, we look for specific information when watching a weather channel to plan a trip or to listen to the sports news to find out the outcome of a game.

Extensive listening means listening to the overall content of a long text, such as a film or a play. Likewise, *intensive listening* means trying to understand all the facts and information – for example, listening to a lecture about which a summary must be written. However, the skills required might change according to the purpose of the listener. If you listen to a lecture only to gain an overall knowledge of the topic, you will not indulge in intensive listening but will only look for the gist or the general meaning.

Listening purpose is an important variable. The processes and strategies employed by the listener change according to his or her purpose. Listening to a sequence of instructions for installing new computer software requires different skills and strategies than listening to a poem or a short story. Therefore, when designing learning tasks, it is important to teach students a range of listening strategies and skills.

Classroom listening activities are broadly divided into two categories: *Language analysis tasks* (language for perception) and *Language use tasks* (language for comprehension).

Language analysis tasks (language for perception)
The aim of these tasks is to give opportunities to analyze selected aspects of both language structure and language use. These tasks also encourage the development of some listening strategies to facilitate learning. Actual comprehension is a secondary consideration and emphasis is on aural perception. Activities can focus on one or two points at a time and would include focus on a variety of features of grammar, pronunciation, vocabulary, discourse markers, sociolinguistic features, and strategic features (Canale & Swain, 1980). Specific activities can include the following:

1. analysis of some of the features of "fast speech" through the use of tasks that will help students learn to cope with rapid, natural, contextualized speech

2. analysis of phrasing and pausing points can be used to facilitate listening as well as "chunking" the input into units for interpretation
3. analysis of both monologue "speeches" and dialogue exchanges with attention to discourse organizational structures
4. describing and analyzing sociolinguistic dimensions, including participants and their roles and relationships, settings, purpose of the communication and its expected outcomes
5. describing and analyzing communicative strategies used by speakers to deal with miscommunication, communication breakdowns, and distractions (Morley, 1991)

Other activities may include identifying word divisions, identifying stress and unstress, identifying intonation, dictation, repetition, etc.

Language use tasks (language for comprehension)
The aim of these tasks is to give students practice in listening to get information and to use it communicatively. These activities help learners to comprehend and use language in order to communicate effectively. Specific activities can include the following:

1. listening and performing actions (Simon Says, etc.)
2. listening and performing operations (constructing a figure, drawing a map, etc.)
3. listening and solving problems (riddles, puzzles, etc.)
4. listening and transcribing (taking notes, etc.)
5. listening and summarizing information (giving the gist of a message, etc.)
6. interactive listening and negotiating meaning through questioning answering routines (to get repetition of information, to verify information, to clarify information, questioning to get elaboration)   (Morley, 1991)

These listening and language use tasks help students to build on their background knowledge in the second language as well as build strategies to facilitate successful communication. In short, all the above activity types help students to develop both top-down and bottom-up processing of information, which is essential in building effective listening skills and strategies.

Assessment of Listening Skills
The method used for assessing listening skills depends on the purpose of assessment. A method that is appropriate for evaluating students at the end of the course is not appropriate to the test taken to give constructive feedback to students while they are engaged in learning a new skill. Moreover, assessments used by teachers must be valid, reliable, and fair.

There are different types of assessments that can be used to evaluate students' learning of skills and strategies based on the purpose of the assessment. Selecting an appropriate instrument for assessment depends on the purpose of the assessment and the given situation. If the purpose of the test is to assess a specific set of skills, students' strengths and weaknesses at the beginning of the course, or students' mastery of a specific skill, the test should assess only those skills. However, if the purpose of the test is to assess distinct goals, then it should measure progress over time. The use of a variety of assessment tools is an important element to consider as well.

Typically, during a listening test, students listen to a passage and then answer multiple-choice questions that assess various levels of literal and inferential comprehension. The important aspects of a listening comprehension test are the listening stimuli, the questions, and the test environment. It is important that the listening stimuli should model the language the students are expected to encounter in the classroom, in various media, or in conversations. In order to engage the students, the passage should be relatively short and interesting. Furthermore, the topic of the passage should be based on experiences common to all students. Any kind of bias should be avoided, for example, material slanted for or against one sex, or a particular geographic, socioeconomic, or racial/ethnic background.

Additionally, multiple-choice items should focus only on the most important aspect of the passage and should measure a specific set of skills. Students should not have to rely upon prior knowledge or experience to answer the questions. However, an alternative to a selected-response test is a performance test that requires students to select a picture or perform a task based on oral instruction. For example, students might hear a description of a few scenes and choose pictures that match the description or they might be given a map and asked to follow a route described orally.

Finally, the testing environment for listening assessment should be free of external distractions. If stimuli are presented from a recording, the sound quality is of importance. If a test administrator presents stimuli, the material should be presented clearly, with an appropriate volume and rate of speaking.

Skill 4.5 **Selects appropriate classroom speaking activities (e.g., paired and small- group conversations, choral speaking, creative drama, role playing, incorporation of digital media and data in presentations) and supports English Language Learners with scaffolded materials and appropriate instructional strategies to meet learning standards related to speaking and to extend students' communicative competence and social interaction skills**

The teaching of speaking skills has moved away from a focus on perfect accuracy towards a focus on fluency and communicative effectiveness. This has affected the kind of activities used by the teachers in the classroom. These communicative activities promote students' ability to understand and communicate real information. They also provide opportunities for them to engage in interaction that is as close as possible to real life situations.

For beginning students, Total Physical Response by Asher (1982) allows ELLs to participate without forcing speech in the beginning of their introduction to the English Language. TPR consists of the instructor issuing commands that are carried out by the students using high-quality pictures to illustrate concepts or vocabulary. The popular children's game *Simons Says* can be used after vocabulary items have been introduced in the classroom for a slightly different way to achieve the same goals.

Krashen and Terrell (1983) developed the Natural Approach. In addition to active involvement and comprehensible input, learners start by making simple choices, answering yes-no questions, and playing games. Students are introduced to new vocabulary by different experiences. Similarly, the Language Experience Approach (LEA) is an instructional technique used to encourage spoken responses from ELL students after they are exposed to a variety of first-hand sensory experiences (Badia, 1966). LEA develops and improves the students' reading and writing skills by using their ideas and language.

The Cognitive Academic Language Learning Approach (CALLA) launched by Chamot and O'Malley (1994) helps intermediate and advanced students understand and retain content area material as they are enhancing their English language skills. CALLA helps ELLs by giving instruction in the appropriate language areas (specialized vocabulary, syntax, phonology) while dealing with different content areas. Learning strategies that emphasize critical and creative thinking skills such as problem solving, inferencing, etc., need to be taught during these lessons since they are critical to success in the mainstream classroom.

Additionally, it is critical to provide students with comprehensible input which is just above their proficiency level. For example, for beginning students, this would be in the form of short sentences, phrases, and relatively simple language segments which are integrated into activities of purposeful communication. These exchanges should be as authentic as possible and carried out in a meaningful context (activity/task). These activities and tasks can be adjusted to the levels and needs of the ELLs. **(See 3.1)**

The selection of appropriate activities depends on the level of the learners. For example, beginning level students need more controlled, structured practice and drills to move to slightly more complex communicative activities. On the other hand, advanced learners may be asked to engage in less structured activities on their own. Following are the examples of the kinds of activities that could promote speaking skills.

Linguistically Structured Activities
Structured activities for beginning ELLs can promote confidence in speaking and accuracy at the same time. Using clearly structured activities provides a form that novice English speakers can imitate and repeat in simple communication. Such controlled activities can be provided with a context, so they could have some of the elements of a communicative activity. This would help the beginner level student focus on accurate structure within a communicative context. An example of this is the structured interview, where students question each other and answer, exchanging real

information while at the same time repeating and producing specific structures (e.g., yes-no, or where/when/who questions).

Some language games can also provide students with controlled practice. However, it is important to model the language structures for the beginning students. Games can help students focus on and repeat specific structures as well as perform natural, "authentic" tasks.

Performance Activities

In performance activities, language learners prepare for the activity beforehand and, for example, deliver a message to a group. This could vary from students' speech explaining an experiment to simply telling a story from their own experience. The follow-up activity could involve videotaping the students during their performances and having them evaluate themselves. This allows the students to focus on communication during their initial performance and in the follow-up session to deal with specific language features. This follow-up self-evaluation can promote greater accuracy in future while the initial activity allows students to focus on the ideas they wish to communicate. Additionally, role play and dramas can be used for all language learners making varying demands on the learners according to their proficiency level. Finally, the spontaneous responses required of debate can also be an effective performance activity for intermediate and advanced learners.

Participation Activities

Participation activities allow students to participate in some communication activity in a natural setting. One of these activities is the guided discussion, where the teacher introduces a problem or a controversial topic. Students in small groups discuss the problem and try to come up with appropriate solutions. For more advanced classes, students could choose a topic and then lead a discussion on it. This activity helps with elements ranging from turn-taking, to topic control amongst the students, as well as accuracy of grammar and pronunciation. Another activity is the interview, where students interview a native speaker about some meaningful or memorable experience in their lives. After the interview, the students organize the information collected to present it to the whole class.

Observation Activities

These are activities in which students record both verbal and nonverbal interactions between native speakers or advanced speakers of the target language. This helps students become aware of the language spoken in an authentic setting. It also allows students to observe how people greet each other, make requests, interrupt each other, respond to each other, disagree, or receive compliments. A follow-up activity could be a role play created by the students to show the verbal and nonverbal behaviors appropriate in a particular situation.

To enhance communicative competence, it is paramount to provide students with a relaxed classroom environment in which they feel comfortable and confident. It allows the students to take risks and produces more interactions. The teacher should also provide the students with situations as close as possible to real life in which they can communicate with one another. The speaker's focus is on the communicative task itself, for which they collaborate to achieve mutual understanding and modify their language according to the demands of the situation.

Interactive group work is also important to lessen students' anxiety and lower their affective filters. Anxiety can seriously impede the learning process. Different group sizes (pairs, small groups, and large groups) provide opportunities for students to practice the different thinking and oral skills that are unique to each group type. Similarly, when students' affective filter is lowered, they are more likely to take risks and engage in meaningful conversations without the fear of mistakes. Students also develop social skills by interacting in a variety of small group situations that aim to resolve a problem or give directions, advice, etc.

In classrooms where these strategies are in place, the teacher helps students build on what they already know, which helps them expand on their prior knowledge and retain information. Ideally, to promote more complex communication, the questions asked in the class should produce a variety of responses for which there is no right answer. Furthermore, students should be provided with ample opportunities for comprehensible input where meaning is negotiated within a contextualized meaningful context. Some strategies for a communicative classroom could be peer interviews, problem-solving conversations, debates, etc.

Additionally, it is important to provide students with comprehensible input. For instance, for beginner level ESL students, comprehensible input would be in the form of short sentences, phrases, and relatively simple language segments which are integrated into activities of purposeful communication. Similarly, second language learners should communicate in situations/exchanges which are as authentic as possible and should bring about a maximum of personal involvement in the communication.   Students should also be provided opportunities to use the target language in social interactions which allow the students to produce the language in varied contexts.

Skill 4.6   Supports English Language Learners in developing foundational English literacy skills through various strategies including building on home language literacy and explicit instruction in core reading skills

Foundational literacy skills include demonstrating an understanding of print concepts (organization and features of print), phonological awareness (see 1.9 and 1.10), knowing and applying phonics and word recognition (see 1.9 and 1.10) and fluency.

English Language fluency is developed over time through extensive practice both in speaking and in reading. Ample opportunities should be given to ELLs to develop their speaking and listening abilities to help them achieve more oral fluency. Role-playing, skits, poems, singing, and interviews are good ways to increase oral fluency. Fluency in reading interacts with oral fluency. Wide exposure to print and reading will increase both reading fluency and oral fluency. The two are intertwined.

Fluent readers are able to grasp chunks of language, read for meaning (not word by word), decode automatically, and become confident readers who are able to self-monitor, while maintaining comprehension. Specific instruction devoted to these areas should improve fluency rates in slower readers. Promoting first language literacy and drawing connections to developing literacy in English will support ELLs' literacy development.

See 1.4 (instruction in core reading skills) and 4.8 (effective reading instruction)

Skill 4.7   Prioritizes foundational English literacy skills for early stage language learners regardless of age

There may be a temptation to immerse new English Language Learners who are older in content-area English. Because of their age, it may seem unfair or juvenile to teach foundational literacy skills such as word recognition and fluency, but without mastery of these concepts, students will not fulfil their academic potential and high-level literacy will remain a challenge.

Students with strong literacy skills in their first language will most likely move more quickly past the foundational skills in English. For those who do not have those skills in their first language, however, it is pertinent to take the time to ensure students master them. Only through mastery of these skills will students be ready to engage with complex literary texts, read and research for information, or follow complex procedural texts. Ignoring the foundational aspects of literacy does a disservice to ELL students.

Skill 4.8   Demonstrates knowledge of principles and strategies of effective reading instruction

Pressley (2008) discusses the mental processes of good readers and states that teachers need to understand what good reading entails. According to him, good readers rely on both decoding strategies and comprehension strategies to achieve their reading goals. A decoding focused strategy is considered a 'bottom-up' approach while a 'top-down' approach relies more on the reader's prior knowledge and experience. Both these processes should be taught to increase students' reading ability. A third 'interactive model' combines both approaches with readers drawing on both their prior experience and word knowledge to construct meaning (Ahmadi and Pourhossein, 2012).

Teachers should take the following strategies into account to design effective reading instruction programs.

1. *Phonemic awareness*: Phonemes are the smallest units of sound that combine to form syllables and words. For example, the word shut has three phonemes (sh-

u-t) while skip has four phonemes (s-k-i-p). Therefore, phonemic awareness enables the learner to identify and manipulate these phonemes. Some English phonemes may be absent in students' native language and are more difficult to acquire. In this case, it is necessary to teach phonemic awareness with the vocabulary word, its meaning, and its pronunciation. Additionally, teachers could learn about the phonemes that exist or do not exist in their students' first language in order to provide them with effective instruction. Meaningful activities that focus on particular sounds and letters, such as language games and word wall, are useful as are songs and poems that help teach phonemes with rhythm and repetition.

2. *Phonics*: This is the understanding of the relationship between the phonemes and graphemes (the letters and spellings that represent sound in the written language). It helps readers read familiar words and decode unfamiliar ones. Instructional activities that develop students' phonemic awareness help them understand the systematic and predictable relationship between written letters and spoken sounds. Teachers can effectively teach phonics if they have knowledge about their students' native language. For example, in Spanish the letters b, c, d, f, l, m, n, p, q, s, and t represent sounds that are similar enough to English that students may learn them with relative ease. However, the vowels look similar in English and Spanish but are named differently and have different sounds. Therefore, they may be more difficult for Spanish speakers to master when reading English (Peregoy and Boyle, 2000).

3. *Reading fluency*: Reading fluency is crucial for reading comprehension. A fluent reader not only reads words quickly and accurately but also comprehends them at the same time. Students can be taught fluency by reading passages aloud with explicit instruction from the teacher. The other way is for students to read silently on their own with less teacher guidance. However, accent should not be confused with lack of fluency, as students can learn to read fluently in English even with a native language accent.

4. *Vocabulary development*: Vocabulary development is crucial for reading comprehension. It is difficult for a reader to understand the content unless they know the meaning of most of the words in the text. Vocabulary development is particularly important for beginner ELL students both to support comprehension and to avoid frustration. Avoiding frustration will promote a more positive attitude towards reading. When a student sounds out a word, it helps to make sense of the word if they already know its meaning and are able to understand the sentence. Therefore, vocabulary needs to be taught explicitly as a part of the daily curriculum to help ELLs comprehend academic texts.

5. *Reading comprehension strategies*: Comprehension is an active process that requires a repertoire of strategies. These strategies help students engage with the text and monitor their comprehension. Brown (2008) notes that secondary students need a wide variety of strategies in order to tackle the complex reading

required of them to succeed in and out of school. Students need to be taught explicitly how, why, and when to use these strategies. Pearson and Gallagher's Gradual Release of Responsibility Model (1983) for adolescence provides guidance with teaching strategies. Teachers explicitly describe the strategies they use while reading and demonstrate them to the students during read-aloud. Students model these strategies and later adapt them to suit their individual needs. This shifts the focus of responsibility from the teacher to the learner to help them adapt and internalize the strategies.

6. *Scaffolds before, during, and after reading*: "Scaffold" is the term used for teacher support for a learner through dialog, questioning, conversation, and modeling. A number of such reading strategies such as questioning, discussion, and writing are recommended for struggling readers. Roehler and Cantlon (1997) identified five types of scaffolding: (a) offering explanations, (b) inviting student participation, (c) verifying and clarifying student understandings, (d) modeling of desired behaviors, and (e) inviting students to contribute clues for reasoning through an issue or problem. Additionally, these reading strategies/ scaffolding activities should also be used in the content-area classroom in order for them to be effective.

7. *Knowledge about the learner*. Diagnostic assessment is necessary to determine the strengths and weaknesses of the students to provide effective instruction. Knowledge regarding the history of students' reading difficulties would help the teacher focus more on these problematic areas. Similarly, knowledge regarding the cultural and linguistic background of the students assists the teacher in selecting reading material for the class in accordance with their interests, cultural sensitivity, and acknowledgement of their cultural beliefs and values.

Skill 4.9   Applies knowledge of various informational and literary texts and purposes for reading

Literary Texts
Literary genres are collections of works with a similar theme or style. Some literary genres come under the huge umbrella of biography and nonfiction whereas others, like folktales, are further classified into fables, tall tales, fairy tales, and myths. Additionally, under fiction, there are other literary genres: historical fiction, mystery, realistic fiction, fantasy, science fiction, etc. Students should be made aware of these different genres and the different formats and styles that make them distinct. Learning about the features of new text types provides students with additional tools for understanding complex texts. For example, learning that an essay typically starts with the author's main point, continues on to incorporate his/her evidence or arguments, and then ends with a conclusion will help all students (but particularly ELL students) to identify main ideas, look for key points, or even to construct a clear contrary opinion. The concept of genre and its purpose becomes more complicated as children advance to a higher grade level.

Informational Texts and Purposes for Reading

According to Shanahan (2008), people make decisions based on information that comes from multiple viewpoints in multiple formats (e.g., letters, essays, reports, advertisements, lectures) through various media (e.g., newspapers, television, websites, books, magazines). This is evident in content-area subjects as well. For example, historians supply evidence from multiple sources (e.g., film, newspapers, letters, interviews, fictional accounts) to prove their point of view regarding a historical event. The views regarding a particular event might change based on the era in which historians were doing the writing and who the historians were. Historians not only read multiple genres when collecting information but also write them (e.g., scholarly books, journals, articles, lectures). This is also true for other disciplines, such as science and mathematics. Students must also learn to gather information or present their own ideas in different genres and formats.

These multiple genres within a single topic make reading even more challenging for ESL learners. This struggle is magnified when these genres communicate contradictory purposes and messages depending on the author and the context. These genres and their purposes for writing change across disciplines; therefore, teachers need to make students aware of these differences so they can become critical readers. Shanahan (2008) suggests what teachers could do to help students to understand complex texts of different genres:

- Pre-teach potentially troublesome vocabulary.
- Provide information to build background knowledge. Use an anchor text or experience before reading a more difficult text.
- Teach students to use strategies that will help them to better interpret texts. This includes teaching the key features of different text types.
- Teach students about various genres and structures used in particular texts and how texts within those genres signal important information.
- Teach students information about the discipline in which they are reading as well as how experts in that discipline approach and use information in text to build upon existing knowledge.
- Set up cooperating group structures that allow students who are weaker readers to be supported in their reading by better readers.
- Find easier texts or annotate existing texts to make them easier if the difficult texts are challenging and students become unmotivated, even with all of the support they receive.

Skill 4.10 Employs research-based methods and resources to support English Language Learners' achievement in the learning standards related to the evaluation and comprehension of complex informational and literary texts

Critical Literacy: The development of critical literacy skills in English Language Learners can increase levels of achievement in learning standards relating to their understanding of complex informational and literary texts.

The instructor can integrate the following strategies to promote critical literacy for L2 learners:

- Ask the L2 learners to consider the author's motivation for writing a certain newspaper or magazine article. Specifically, ask the learners to support their opinions and answers, using examples of tone, structure, and word choice.
- Ask the L2 learners to compare/contrast the photographs, topics, and writing styles of an L1 and L2 newspaper. Specifically, ask the learners what the style of each may reveal about the different cultures or countries, whether these differences influence readership, and if the choice of advertising influences readership.

The critical piece of both activities is for the learners to not only consider the specific questions, but to also consider which values, ethics, and cultural factors influence their own thinking and responses. Most importantly, instructors need to introduce topics that are relevant to the L2 learner, as well as use codes. "Codes" are graphics, pictures, speeches, themes, issues, or realia from a specific culture that help stimulate discussion. "Simple, familiar, focused representations of complex, often emotionally charged issues or situations, codes can be structured for use with low level learners" (Van Duzer and Florez, 2001). Providing English Language Learners with opportunities to engage with texts that prompt them to examine values, morals, and biases of individuals, groups and the new culture(s) can help promote critical literacy skills.

Graphic Organizers and Mind Maps: Graphic organizers and mind maps can help students evaluate and comprehend more complex informational texts by helping English Language Learners visualize raw data. These can be used by the teacher for simplification of complex materials, numerous data, and complicated relationships in content areas. Students use them to analyze data, organize information, and clarify concepts. Examples are: pie charts, flow charts, bar diagrams, Venn diagrams, family trees, spider maps, organizational charts, and strip maps. Still other graphic organizers are webbing, concept mapping, passwords and language ladders, and brainstorming.

- With webbing, students learn to associate words or phrases within a topic or concept.
- By using concept maps, students learn the relationships between the different elements of a topic and how to organize them from the most general to the most specific. This is different from webbing, where relationships between words or phrases are shown, but not ranked.

Passwords and Language Ladders: Words of the Day and Language Ladders are motivating ways to teach chunks of language to ELLs. The Word of the Day is language needed for daily student life in school. After the words or phrases are explained, they are posted on the board, and must be used before leaving the room or participating in some activity. Language ladders are associated words, such as different ways to say hello or good-bye.

Brainstorming: Brainstorming consists of students contributing ideas related to a concept or problem-centered topic. The teacher initially accepts all ideas without comment. Students then categorize, prioritize, and select proposed ideas for further investigation.

Vocabulary Study: Research has shown that the same 1000 words (approximately) make up 84 percent of the words used in conversation and 74 percent of the words in academic texts (The Nation, 2001). The second most frequently used 1000 words increases the percentage to 90 percent of the words used in conversation and 78 percent of those used in academic texts. The ELL needs to understand 95 percent to achieve comprehension of the academic text. ELLs need to acquire the 2000 most used words and work on academic content words at the same time. In order to help students acquire the vocabulary they need for school, consider the following:

- Vocabulary development for young children is increased using the same methods used with native speaker beginning readers: ample exposure to print, word walls, realia, signs on objects around the room, and so on.
- Older children may take advantage of all these methods in addition to listing true and false cognates, creating personal dictionaries writing in interactive journals with their teachers, and using learning strategies to augment their vocabulary.
- Other strategies from Peregoy and Boyle (2008) are:
  - Activate the prior knowledge of the ELL.
  - Repeat the new word in meaningful contexts.
  - Explore the word in depth through demonstrations, direct experience, concrete examples, and applications to real life.
  - Have students explain concepts and ideas using the new words
  - Provide explicit strategy instruction so that students can independently understand and use the new words.

Reading Comprehension Strategies: Successful readers use reading strategies in each of the three distinct phases of reading—pre-reading, reading, and post-reading—to successfully understand a text (Peregoy and Boyle, 2008). Teachers can use pre, during and post-reading strategies to build English Language Learners' reading comprehension skills.

- Pre-reading: Build background knowledge through anticipation guides or field trips, motivate the reader with structured overviews or films, and establish the purpose using experiments or pictures.
- During reading: Read based upon the established purpose, using learning logs or annotating texts to record information, to improve comprehension by Directed Reading-Thinking Activities and asking questions, and to utilize background knowledge by studying headings and subheadings and answering questions.
- Post-reading: Help the student with organizing and remembering information through activities such as art work, maps, or summaries and to use the information in reporting, making a film, or publishing. (See 4.8).

Skill 4.11 **Applies knowledge of the writing process in designing activities to develop students' writing proficiency while identifying strategies for developing students' organization in writing and their ability to write in different academic genres**

Just as the native English speaker has to manage many different skills to become a proficient writer, so must the ELL student. ELL students must develop clarity of thought and expression, use of different genres for different purposes in writing, and standard conventions of spelling, grammar, and punctuation. Since the characteristics of each type of writing may vary, it is not always easy to discuss writing stages. Students may develop proficiency more quickly in one text type than another. Because of the complexity of learning to express oneself in writing, it is particularly important to have a clear process of writing instruction for students who are simultaneously developing language skills in a new language.

The following set of writing traits with accompanying level descriptors, based on a writing matrix developed by Peregoy and Boyle (2008), offers a good guide to identifying characteristics of an English Language Learner's writing level. It encompasses three developmental levels and six traits.

- Trait 1: Fluency
    - Beginning Level: Writes one or two short sentences.
    - Intermediate Level: Writes several sentences.
    - Advanced Level: Writes a paragraph or more.

- Trait 2: Organization
    - Beginning Level: Lacks logical sequence or is so short that organization presents no problem.
    - Intermediate Level: Somewhat sequenced.
    - Advanced Level: Follows standard organization for genre.

- Trait 3: Grammar
    - Beginning Level: Basic word order problems. Uses only present tense form.
    - Intermediate Level: Minor grammatical errors.
    - Advanced Level: Grammar resembles that of native speaker of same age.

- Trait 4: Vocabulary
    - Beginning Level: Limited vocabulary. Needs to rely at times on L1 or ask for translation.
    - Intermediate Level: Knows most words needed to express ideas, but lacks vocabulary for finer shades of meaning.
    - Advanced Level: Flexible in word choice; similar to good native writer of same age.

- Trait 5: Genre
  - Beginning Level: Does not differentiate form to suit purpose.
  - Intermediate Level: Chooses form to suit purpose but limited in choices of expository forms.
  - Advanced Level: Knows several genres; makes appropriate choices. Similar to effective native writers of the same age.

- Trait 6: Sentence variety
  - Beginning Level: Uses one or two sentence patterns.
  - Intermediate Level: Uses several sentence patterns.
  - Advanced Level: Uses a good variety of sentence patterns effectively.

For beginning level students, the first steps in teaching writing skills in an ESL classroom center around the mechanics of the skill. This means letter recognition, letter discrimination, word recognition, basic rules of spelling, punctuation and capitalization, and recognition of whole sentences and paragraphs. Recognition and writing drills are the initial steps that help in the development of effective writing skills.

Three main types of recognition tasks are usually used at the early stages of learning:

1. **Matching tasks:** These are effective recognition tasks that are mostly in the form of games, puzzles, etc.
2. **Writing tasks:** At this early stage of writing, it is important to get learners accustomed to correct capitalization in English and to basic punctuation rules.
3. **Meaningful sound spelling correspondence practice:** Students write meaningful sentences (accompanied by pictures) that show sound-spelling correspondences. These sentences practice correct capitalization and punctuation rules as well as words that students have recently learned. These sentences may not be interesting but fulfill a definite purpose. Eventually, this language knowledge works as the basis for developing more meaningful and interesting texts.

The next step focuses on the basic process-oriented tasks that incorporate some language at the morphological and discourse level. Therefore, these activities focus on both accuracy and content of the message. This step caters to a wide range of proficiency levels, depending on the specifications of the task. These include:

1. *Practical writing tasks:* These writing tasks have a predictable format, which makes them suitable for focusing primarily on spelling and morphology. These include various types of lists, notes, short messages, simple instructions, etc. This step caters to beginning and intermediate level students.

2. *Emotive writing tasks:* These are concerned with personal writing, which includes letters to friends and narratives describing personal experiences, as well as personal journals and diaries. These writing activities are suitable for intermediate and advanced learners but can also be used at the beginning level

in a limited manner. For example, letters can be limited to the level of structure and vocabulary knowledge of the students as they increase in their proficiency level. It is necessary to provide students with specifications for the tasks in order for them to respond according to their proficiency levels.

3. *School-oriented tasks*: The function of writing in school is the most important aspect of students' writing. A lot of individual learning takes place when students are writing assignments, summaries, answers to questions, book reports, research papers, or a variety of essay-type passages. The teacher could be the audience of these writing tasks, but eventually the students should be engaged in activities that convey information to multiple audiences across multiple genres (Shanahan, 2008). At an early stage of ESL learning, the assignments should be short and limited. Answers might be single phrases or sentences, and summaries could be just listing main ideas. However, at a higher proficiency level, the activities can require more complex structure and organization skills catering to multiple audiences and also skills involving writing across different genres (e.g., research papers, scientific journals and magazines, newspaper articles, etc.).

Appropriate task selection involves a variety of factors, but it is also important to use a variety of writing tasks at all levels of student learning. Writing is a vital communication skill and requires the learner to plan and think about the process. Therefore, the learner focuses on both linguistic accuracy and content organization with these tasks.

In early studies of developing writing skills in all learners, the focus of research was on the product produced by the writer. However, Emig's (1971) L1 research changed the focus from product to process. This has become the focus of the research design for conducting research in both L1 and L2 writing process. Similar to Emig's research, L2 composition specialists Zamal (1976) and Raimes (1979) recommended treating L2 writing as a process in the L2 classroom. This approach focuses less on surface-level errors and achieving correctness, but stresses process-oriented pedagogy. In a process-oriented writing class, the teacher provides students with a wide range of strategies for composing texts. This approach focuses on what the writer does (planning, revising, etc.) instead of only what the final product looks like (grammar, spelling, etc.).

One way of addressing different language levels is to characterize writing tasks along a continuum from *controlled* to *guided* to *free* which starts with maximum teacher-controlled activities and builds to tasks that require students to supply content, organization, and language structure. A controlled task may require students to make changes to an existing text or to write based on teacher-supplied model text. An example of a guided writing task, which allows more freedom to the student than a controlled task, is to ask students to produce a short text by answering directed yet open-ended questions.

Finally, free writing tasks ask students to produce complete texts in response to a variety of writing prompts. Free writing can also be encouraged with less emphasis on the correctness of grammar or form by having students keep a journal.

The focus of all writing should be to allow students to learn and practice the skills of producing good writing. Regardless of the kind of writing task, prewriting is important at the beginning. The goal of the teacher should be to present students with a variety of prewriting strategies and help them figure out which one works best for them for the task. Some examples are:

- brainstorming
- listing
- free writing
- clustering

After this first step, the teacher needs to work with students to help them revise and improve their original written task, especially at the free writing stage. This drafting process is an essential part of the writing process where students learn to revise and to work through a series of drafts before considering a paper finished. Knowledge of a student's writing level for particular traits can help guide instruction. Mini-lessons, one-on-one instruction, and individualized goals can help ELL students address specific elements of their writing in different genres and styles.

Another stage that requires a lot of attention is responding to student writing. This is a complex process which requires teachers to develop or adopt strategies which help foster student improvement. Moreover, students should also be trained to use the feedback in ways that will improve their writing. This feedback should not only be on surface level errors but on the relevance of the idea to the topic and also on strategies students should utilize in producing better essays. These strategies should be taught explicitly to the students (prewriting, revising, organizing, etc.) for them to implement during the writing process. There are many ways of providing teacher feedback:

- Oral teacher feedback in the form of individual or group conferences
- Written comments or suggestions on students' drafts
- Modelling the traits of good writing using exemplars or model texts
- Peer response in which students read or listen to each other's papers for the purpose of providing insight. This could be done in groups or pairs. The teacher can provide guidelines to the students so they remain focused on the task at hand.

The above stages are important in the writing process and should be implemented effectively by the teacher. The writing of the composition as well as the feedback stage of the writing process are crucial in improving the writing abilities of all learners but especially those developing fluency in English.

To keep students engaged in a writing task, it is important for the writer to be interested in the task. Therefore, these tasks need a purpose other than just *language practice*. Personal topics (such as autobiography, hobbies, preferences, problems) allow students to convey real information. However, when topics move away from personal narratives, it is helpful to specify the communicative purpose of the topic. A topic like, "A vacation on a cruise ship is a wonderful experience" can be changed to "Write an advertisement for a cruise ship to convince people to take a cruise." While selecting a topic, it is necessary to consider how to make it meaningful for both the reader and the writer. This way the writer will put more effort and interest into his/her writing in order to communicate a real meaning.

Skill 4.12   Uses research based methods to support English Language Learners' production of text-based written responses and research based writing projects

The organization of written discourse in English is culturally determined, to a large degree. Therefore, students who write well in their first language cannot simply rely solely on their prior writing skills when writing in English. Students have to learn not only how English sentences are formed but also how paragraphs and longer pieces are constructed. In written English, we generally state our topic and elaborate on our statement by adding supporting details such as facts, examples, descriptions, illustrations, reasons, causes, effects, comparisons, and contrasts.

Additionally, multiple texts are used across all subject areas to convey "multiple viewpoints in multiple formats (e.g., letters, essays, reports, advertisements, lectures), through various venues (e.g., newspapers, television, postcards, websites, books, magazines)..." (Shanahan, 2008). Shanahan (2008) further postulates that adolescents need instruction to use effective strategies in writing about the same topic in multiple ways and for multiple purposes. Students need to learn to keep the audience in mind as well as the kind of writing they are engaged in. They can use the techniques mentioned below to help them identify these factors beforehand.

Organizing thoughts in writing is a process in itself. A number of strategies can be used to teach students these skills. They allow the students to make choices with the purpose of the task in mind. Following are some techniques that would help students develop organization skills.

1. Outlines
There are two basic types of outlines:

- An outline the writer makes before writing the text
- An outline the writer makes of what he has already written

An outline that is developed before writing the text should be brief and made after extensive discussion, list-making, brainstorming, and other prewriting activities. It helps to guide the writer in developing the text. Similarly, an outline that is made after the first draft is written helps the writer analyze his/her work and see what needs to be done to make the text clearer to the reader. A technique to teach this skill would be to give the students a reading passage and ask them either to discuss and make their own outline of what has been written or to complete the skeleton of a given outline.

2. Analysis

Outlining is one way to help students examine a text closely. Additionally, students should analyze a reading passage and ask questions about a piece of writing regarding not only what the writer has written but also how s/he has written it. Some techniques to teach this skill are: (a) Students are given short paragraphs and asked to read one sentence of each. Then they are asked to discuss in pairs or in groups which one sentence best expresses the paragraph it belongs to and why. (b) Give or read students a paragraph without its topic sentence or the concluding sentence. Then ask the students to choose from the choices provided and give reasons for their choice. If the students are advanced, they could discuss the passage and write their own sentences.

3. Models

Model paragraphs or texts should not be used for students to imitate mechanically, but they should be used as a resource for the writer. For example, the students might read a passage comparing two bicycles and then write their own composition comparing two cars, following the organizational and structural pattern of the model. Explicit instruction that draws attention to the features of specific text types will help students learn the features of important forms like essays, research projects, etc. Rather than following the model step-by-step, students use their prior analysis of the form as a resource to help deal with problems that may emerge in the process of their own writing. For example, if the student is not sure how to best organize an argument, the model can be used to analyze, manipulate, and shed a light on what path to take.

Research based projects are extremely important both as a writing form and for success in different academic disciplines. Completing research projects can pose additional challenges for English Language Learners because of the reading and analysis required to complete them. Integrating information gleaned from different sources into a project can be particularly difficult for students in the early stages of vocabulary and literacy development in English.

Teachers can support students as they address the challenges of researching a topic by assisting them in selecting texts, curating resources that are directly connected to the project, or by helping students break down key information within a text. These scaffolding strategies should be used with the goal of helping the learner move towards independence. These strategies can be targeted to support students with the challenges of reading or to allow them to focus on the process of writing, depending on the teacher's perception of student need.

(See also 4.11)

Skill 4.13 Applies instructional strategies that address conventions of English grammar, usage, and mechanics

There has been a lot of discussion regarding the role of grammar in the teaching of writing. Research has shown grammar to be an aid for language users to effectively communicate their ideas and to make meaning clear and precise. Therefore, the purpose of the teacher is not to teach grammar for error correction but to use it to address specific needs of the students and to develop appropriate instructional materials for learners at all stages of the writing process. It is important to include grammar-oriented activities not only to help students edit errors in their writing but also to help them understand how grammar contributes to meaning (Frodesen, 1991). Following are the specific strategies and techniques to help achieve this goal.

1. *Text analysis* can allow ELL students to see how particular grammatical features are used to write a particular kind of text in order to communicate the writer's purpose. It also helps writers understand and use appropriate grammatical structures such as definite and indefinite articles, restrictive and nonrestrictive clauses, and present perfect and past or present tense verb forms. However, these exercises should usually be kept short because the real focus of a writing class is to improve the writing skills of the ESL students. The goal should be to identify and explain the functions of grammatical structures in discourse contexts.

2. *Guided writing practice* - The focus of guided writing is on a particular grammatical structure in order to address the grammar problems of learners that are prevalent in their writing. This helps build confidence in ESL learners to use particular grammatical structures that they find difficult and to develop syntactic complexity in their writing. However, guided writing activities are now used not simply as grammar practice but as components of the prewriting, revising, and editing stages of the writing process. Some examples are:
   - Dictation: Dictation can help students diagnose and correct errors in grammar.
   - Text elicitation: The teacher specifies both a topic and grammatical construction/constructions to be used. Student employ these constructions when responding to a writing prompt.
   - Text conversion: Students are given paragraphs or short texts to rewrite, changing some feature of the grammatical structure, for example present tense to past tense. These activities should be as relevant as possible to actual writing. One way of doing this is to use texts that are good models of the text type students are working towards mastering (essay, short story, op-ed piece, etc.).
   - Text completion: Two common types of these activities are the cloze passage and the gapped text.

3. *Editing*
   The focus of these activities is to develop students' abilities to detect and correct errors so they become effective editors of their own writing.
   - Error detection/ Correction exercises: These activities are designed to help students identify and correct the kinds of errors frequently made in their writing, and help intermediate and advanced writers develop systematic strategies for writing. Therefore, whenever possible and appropriate, students' actual text should be used for this task.
   - Read-aloud techniques: During this activity, students read their papers aloud, listen to errors, and correct them as they proceed. Students can also work in pairs and help each other make the corrections.

4. *Teacher correction and feedback on errors*:
   Teachers should help students identify and correct frequent error patterns and devise ways for students to observe improvement in their own work over a short period of time. The Blue Sheet, is an example of an error correction strategy, suggested by Celce-Murcia and Hilles (1988). In this strategy, the teacher attaches a blue sheet with each student's paragraph or essay on which two errors are listed that need immediate attention. This is followed by guided practice in correcting these errors in the classroom.

Additionally, teacher-student conferences can provide more individualized help with grammar problems in writing. It can be done in small groups as well. This helps the teacher take up the role of a collaborator and helps students set goals for improvement and suggest effective correction strategies to one another.

Skill 4.14   Demonstrates knowledge of evidence-based methods for supporting students' acquisition, development and progress in meeting English vocabulary learning standards

Research continues to highlight the role that vocabulary development plays in English language literacy and subject-based learning. ESOL teachers can use evidence-based methods to guide them in vocabulary instruction such as:

- Teaching vocabulary every day in all parts of the curriculum in all four of the learning modalities (reading, writing, listening, speaking)
- Ensuring that words studied are meaningful to students
- Providing plenty of time after introducing words for review, practice and use;
- Identifying words within reading programs that need more intensive instruction for English Language Learners;
- Working with other teachers at grade level or subject area when designing important vocabulary lessons and/or reading about evidence-based approaches to vocabulary instruction;
- Ensuring that reading vocabulary lists emphasize important words and not just decoding;

- Working to create some word lists that are common to many subjects, and if not, making word lists available to subject-area teachers to help students practice;
- Striving to teach short and intensive word lists that are meaningful, rather than longer lists that cannot be truly learned (this can be per week or per day); and
- Teaching conversational/social words as well as academic - English Language Learners need both

Skill 4.15   Selects or creates appropriate assessments and methods (formative and summative) for English Language Learners' various aspects of language development to assist in planning in instruction and/or interventions

Assessment plays several key roles in learning. Aside from measuring progress, assessment provides opportunities to give feedback to students so that they can play an active role in their own learning. With clear information about their progress in English language development, for example, ELL students can set goals, choose strategies for success, and monitor their progress.

For the teacher, assessment is essential in planning instruction and intervention and for communicating effectively with students and their families. With individualized information about students, teachers can target instruction around skills and concepts for those who need them, provide challenge opportunities, and help students work towards personalized goals. If interventions are necessary, the information gathered from formal and informal assessments can be used to document and justify need for additional support for students.

Assessment can take many forms, both formal and informal, formative and summative. Selecting the right type of assessment for the right situation and to get the right type of information works best when the teacher takes a long-term view of what s/he wants to do with the assessment data.

Assessment of oral proficiency
Assessment of speaking skills should evaluate the communicative ability of the English language learner. Rather than focusing on the number of errors an ELL student might make, assessment should emphasize the student's overall ability to communicate ideas clearly. If there are errors in grammar, for example, but the overall message is clear, a student could still do well on the assessment. The errors may be an area for future growth but not a cause of 'failure'. Assessment methods that focus on the message conveyed by the learners are more accurate in evaluating oral proficiency.

There are formal and informal methods to assess oral proficiency of English Language Learners. For example, in the usual classroom setting, students deliver a speech and the teacher gives feedback, using an evaluation form. However, more is required than one-time student evaluation and teacher performance of errors and other features. Peer evaluation is another method of assessment of speaking skills. For example, student evaluators might outline the main points of a presentation in order to demonstrate their ability to follow the speech. The student evaluators can orally sum up their reactions to the performance before the rest of the class. They fill out evaluation forms provided by the teacher for the presenter to read and consider. Other students in the class also fill out the evaluation forms and ask the presenter follow-up questions. These evaluation sheets are used by the teacher as part of the assessment.

Another method of assessment of speaking skills is self-evaluation. With all the digital media tools available for project-based work, this is particularly easy. This method involves recording students during their initial performances and allowing them to evaluate themselves. Students listen to or watch their recorded projects and evaluate themselves according to the same criteria that the teacher and peer evaluators use. After that, the student performers select a portion of their talk and transcribe it in detail. In their initial performance, they focus on communication but at this point, they focus on problems and try to make their speech more effective. At this stage, the teacher could focus on both fluency and accuracy so students could understand that both are important for effective communication. These evaluations could be used in various types of classroom activities, helping students gain confidence in their own ability to evaluate language. This method also leads to an opportunity for real spontaneous interactions as the evaluation process is discussed among the students and is important to everyone involved.

Apart from these informal methods of assessment, there are some formal methods to evaluate students in terms of general oral proficiency. There are testing instruments that focus on the message produced by the students. Apart from this one-time assessment, there are other summative assessments that focus on different types of skills needed to convey a message. For this purpose, many task types are used, such as describing a picture or diagram, giving directions, storytelling, expressing opinions, etc., according to the purpose of the assessment.

Portfolio assessment intends to examine students' oral abilities over an extended period of time. The purpose is to produce a record of each student's progress on a variety of tasks over the course of a given unit of study. This type of assessment could also serve as a diagnostic measure of students' major strengths and weaknesses. The tasks may include describing a picture, summarizing orally, interviews, information gap, role plays, etc. To create a complete profile of the students' performance, a number of different tasks are included.

In these assessments, it is extremely important that students have the opportunity to practice and be familiar with a particular evaluation technique before being evaluated. Likewise, the teacher should also be familiar with the evaluation criteria of each technique used. In short, a variety of techniques should be utilized in order to evaluate students' overall performance.

Reading

Reading involves a complex interplay of skills. Readers have to decode words, derive meaning, anticipate or infer meaning, and make predictions. Evaluating a student's reading level should provide information that can be used to help the student improve or help teachers plan instruction/intervention.

See 3.9 and 3.10 for additional explanations and examples of performance based, conferencing, and other types of formative, summative, informal and formal assessments.

COMPETENCY 5   INSTRUCTING ENGLISH LANGUAGE LEARNERS IN THE CONTENT AREAS

Skill 5.1   **Demonstrates knowledge of state standards and evidence-based methods to help English Language Learners develop both general and content-area language skills; utilizes strategies for selecting and adapting content-area curricula to meet the cognitive and linguistic needs of English language learners**

Teachers should be familiar with the NY State New Language Arts Progressions (formerly English as a Second Language Standards) found at the Engage NY website: (https://www.engageny.org/resource/new-york-state-bilingual-common-core-initiative)

The New York State Bilingual Common Core Initiative has at its core a belief that language-learning proficiency encompasses the language specific to various disciplines as well as mastering grammar structures and vocabulary. When students learn ways of thinking as well as ways of talking about big ideas supported by rich, supporting content in specific texts, they will achieve more in the content area and in language learning in general.

To select and adapt content-area curricula to meet the cognitive and linguistic needs of English Language Learners, teachers can:

- Break down the content so that it is easier to process by providing students with graphic organizers for note-taking, researching, analyzing, planning and assessing (depending on the proficiency level of the English Language Learner and the complexity and type of content);
- Provide different types of vocabulary scaffolds for different levels of proficiency, ranging from more structured to more independent;
- Use formative assessments consistently to determine if English Language Learners are on the path to meeting proficiency goals, and if not, make scaffolding adaptations for individual students and, when necessary, adapt teacher instruction; and
- Pre-teach big-idea vocabulary for specific content areas. This helps students learn the content-area language while also teaching them the different ways of thinking in content-rich subjects such as Social Studies/History, the Sciences and English Language Arts.

(For additional information on adapting content-area curricula see Skill 3.6)

Skill 5.2   **Prioritizes foundational content, knowledge and skills for English Language Learners appropriate to grade and proficiency level**

The growing number of students learning English as a second or additional language has resulted in an increasing demand on all teachers and classrooms to meet the needs of these students, which includes both content and language teachers. Recent research in this area has come up with useful insights that can be applied across both grade level and language classroom settings in order to support ESL students' English language and literacy development. Language and literacy development is the key objective of all grade level curricula to ensure success both inside and outside of the school setting.

These insights can be synthesized into seven key instructional criteria for designing and conducting instruction to support English Language Learners' language and literacy development (Enright, 1991).

1. *Collaboration:* Instruction should be organized for students to have many opportunities to interact and work cooperatively with each other and with teachers, family members, and community members. During collaborative activities, teachers and students actively work together in order for learning to take place. This cooperation entails organizing learning activities which require communicating and sharing, such as discussion groups, student partners, or student-teacher dialogue journals. Collaborative activities also include interacting with people outside of the classroom, such as interviewing the school drama club for the class newspaper or working with a parent or an elder to report on a special family tradition.

2. *Purpose:* Instruction is organized so that students have multiple opportunities to use authentic oral and written language to complete tasks and have real-life goals and purposes. An example of purposeful composition and questioning activities would be students writing letters to city officials to invite them to a class election forum and then interviewing them about school issues. In addition to this, there are four major kinds of purposeful discourse that can be used as learning activities across the curriculum. These are: (a) *shared discourse* in which language is used socially to communicate and share meaning in order to accomplish social goals (playing games or planning a short scene), (b) *fun discourse* in which language is used for fun (singing songs and writing riddles), (c) *fact discourse* in which language is used to get new information and concepts (doing a research project), (d) *thought discourse* in which language is used to imagine and create new ideas and experiences (writing poetry or critical thinking). These discourse features ensure that students learn both language and content with clear goals in mind.

3. *Student interest:* Instruction is organized to both promote and follow students' interest. This does not mean that the instructional goals are changed, but the focus is on organizing activities that combine students' interests and purposes with curriculum topics and objectives.

4. *Previous experience:* Instruction is organized to include students' previous experiences in the new learning. This includes tapping students' previous language and literacy experiences in their first language and English and also their already-developed knowledge and cultural experiences. This approach

entails relating new concepts and materials to students' background experiences, such as brainstorming ideas before reading a text or connecting previous class activities and learning to new ones. An example would be including histories and folk tales from ESL students' families and native countries in reading group instruction or having students collect authentic speech and literacy data from their homes and neighborhoods to be studied in class.

5. *Support:* Instruction is organized so students feel comfortable and take risks in using English. The classroom atmosphere should be supportive, which provides challenging but safe opportunities for students to learn English. The activities are adapted to students' current language and literacy capabilities or *zones of proximal development* (Vygotsky, 1978) in the second language, which also provides scaffolding of the newly acquired skills.

6. *Variety:* Instruction is organized to include a variety of learning activities and language forms and uses. This means that students are exposed to a wide range of oral and written English that they are expected to use in the classrooms and their daily lives. Organization for variety includes the instructional practices of collaboration, learning purposes, student interests, and familiar and unfamiliar student experiences within classroom learning activities.

7. *Integration:* Instruction is organized to integrate the various programs and resources available for supporting ELLs' language and literacy development so that they complement each other. This may include integrating the students' in-school and out-of-school experiences; integrating content and language instruction; integrating the four language skills of reading, writing, listening, and speaking; and integrating the students within the classroom through cooperative learning.

Furthermore, Enright (1991) puts forward modifications in *teacher talk* that could help make language accessible to the students. Krashen and Terrell (1983) refer to it as *comprehensible input* which is just beyond ELL students' current language capabilities. There are various ways in which language teachers and content area teachers can adapt their own classroom discourse to make it comprehensible and useful:

- *Nonverbal adaptations:* This includes gestures, nonverbal illustrations of meanings, and facial expressions.
- *Contextual adaptations:* This includes *visual aids* (e.g., pictures, blackboard sketches, real-life objects) and *auditory aids* (e.g., recorded sounds or recorded speech).
- *Paraverbal adaptations:* Teachers speak more clearly, slowing down the rate of their speech, pausing between major idea units, and varying their volume and intonation to convey meaning.
- *Discourse adaptations:* Teachers use organizational markers, such as *now* and *first*, to make their discourse more comprehensible. They also rephrase their utterances and repeat their utterances in meaningful ways.

- *Elicitation adaptations:* Teachers use a variety of techniques to call on students to ensure student involvement. For example, they call on students by name, they call for volunteers to respond, they call on the whole group, and they have open elicitations where anyone can speak.
- *Questioning adaptations:* Teachers vary their questions according to the proficiency level of the students. For limited English proficiency students, the question could be a sketch or a one- word elicitation, whereas it could be more complicated as the proficiency level progresses.
- *Response adaptations:* Teachers adapt their responses to students' utterances to provide further comprehensible input and to encourage further language use by using *confirmation checks* and *clarification requests.* Teachers rephrase students' responses to provide further information on the topic. Teachers also encourage student response by giving them more *wait time* between the question and the response, through *prompting,* and through *repeating* the response.
- *Correction adaptations:* Teachers correct student responses by focusing on the meaning conveyed, by modeling the correct answer, or by explicitly showing the student his/her error and providing corrective feedback individually or away from the group.

With a combination of these principles, insights, teacher-adaptations and learning activities, teachers can help English Language Learners increase foundational content, knowledge and skills.

Skill 5.3   Recognizes the relationship between language and content-area objectives and employs research-based methods (including collaboration between the ESOL and content-area teachers) to integrate them

It is important, particularly when second language learners have multiple teachers, such as in middle or high school, that teachers communicate and collaborate in order to provide a great level of consistency. It is particularly difficult for second language learners to go from one class to the next, where there are different sets of expectations and varied methods of instruction, and still focus on the more complex elements of learning language.

When students have higher levels of anxiety regarding the learning of a second language, they are less likely to focus on the language; rather, they focus on whatever is creating their anxiety. This does not mean that standards and expectations should be different for these students in all classes; it simply means that teachers should have common expectations so that students know what to expect in each class and don't have to think about the differences between classes.

Another emphatic reason for teachers to collaborate, particularly with the ESOL specialists, is to ensure that students are showing consistent development across classes. Where there is inconsistency, teachers should work to uncover what it is that is keeping the student from excelling in a particular class. In a cooperative teaching environment, the ESOL teacher might work with the classroom or subject-area teacher to develop curriculum and instructional strategies that best meet the needs of all students. Collaborative or partnership teaching "builds on the concept of cooperative teaching by linking the work of two teachers, or indeed a whole department/year team or other partners, with plans for curriculum development and staff development across the school" (Bourne, 1997: 83).

There are a number of essential elements for effective collaboration between language and content-area teachers which have been discussed elsewhere (see, for example, Davison, 1992; Hurst and Davison, 2005), including the need to establish a clear conceptualization of the task, the incorporation of explicit goals for ESL development into curriculum and assessment planning processes, the negotiation of a shared understanding of ESL and mainstream teachers' roles/responsibilities, the adoption of common curriculum planning policies and processes, experimentation with diversity as a resource to promote effective learning for all students, the development of articulated and flexible pathways for ESL learning support, and the establishment of systematic mechanisms for monitoring, evaluation and feedback (Davison, 2001).

Academic tasks tend to increase their cognitive demands as students progress in their schooling, but the context becomes increasingly reduced. ELLs who have not developed Cognitive Academic Language Proficiency or CALP (see 5.4 for more detail) need additional teacher support to achieve success. Contextual support in the form of realia, demonstrations, pictures, graphs, etc. provide the ELL with scaffolding and reduce the language difficulty level of the task. Both content and ESOL teachers should incorporate teaching academic skills in their lessons. The following are essential elements to include in teaching academic English:

1. Integrate listening, speaking, reading, and writing skills in all lessons for all proficiencies.
2. Teach the components and processes of reading and writing.
3. Focus on vocabulary development.
4. Build and activate prior knowledge.
5. Teach language through content and themes.
6. Use native language strategically.
7. Pair technology with instruction.
8. Motivate ELLs with choice.

Skill 5.4 Demonstrates knowledge of discourse features of different text types in various content areas

Discourse
The term discourse refers to linguistic units composed of several sentences and is derived from the concept of "discursive formation" or communication that involves specialized knowledge of various kinds. Conversations, arguments, or speeches are types of discourses. Discourse shapes the way language is transmitted, and also how we organize our thoughts.

The structure of discourse varies among languages and traditions. For example, Japanese writing does not present the main idea at the beginning of an essay; rather, writing builds up to the main idea, which is presented or implied at the end of the essay. This is completely different than English writing, which typically presents the main idea or thesis at the beginning of an essay and repeats it at the end.

In addition to language and structure, topic or focus affects discourse. The discourse in various disciplines approaches topics differently, such as feminist studies, cultural studies, and literary theory. Discourse plays a role in all spoken and written language, and affects our thinking.

Written discourse ranges from the most basic grouping of sentences to the most complicated essays and stories. Regardless of the level, English writing demands certain structure patterns. A typical paragraph begins with a topic sentence which states directly or indirectly the focus of the paragraph, adds supporting ideas and details, and ends with a concluding sentence that relates to the focus and either states the final thought on that topic or provides a transition to the next paragraph when there are more than one. As with spoken discourse, organization, tone, and word choice are critical to transferring thoughts successfully and maintaining interest.

As skills increase, paragraphs are combined into stories or essays. Each type of writing has specific components and structures. Story writing requires setting, plot, and character. Initially, following a chronological order is probably easiest for ELLs, but as learners become more skillful, other types of order should be practiced, such as adding descriptions in spatial order or using flashbacks in a story.

Teachers frequently rely on the standard three- or five-paragraph essay to teach essay writing because it provides a comprehensible structure for organizing and expanding ideas within a single focus. It mirrors the paragraph structure organizationally in that the first, introductory paragraph provides the main idea or focus of the essay, each body paragraph adds and develops a supporting idea and details, and the concluding paragraph provides a summary or other type of conclusion that relates to the main idea or focus stated in the first paragraph. For English Language Learners, the structure of the 3-5 paragraph essay teaches the basic organizational concept of English essay writing. By offering strictly defined limits, the teacher reduces the number of variables to learn about essay writing. Starting with a blank page can be overwhelming for ELLs. Working within this structure enables learners to focus on developing each paragraph, a challenging enough task when one considers the language skills required. As learners become better able to control their writing and sustain a focus, variations can be introduced and topics expanded.

Academic discourse refers to formal academic learning. This includes all the four skills: listening, reading, speaking, and writing. Academic learning is important in order for students to succeed in school. Cummins differentiated between two types of language proficiency: basic interpersonal communication skills (BICS) and cognitive academic language proficiency (CALP). According to research, an average student can acquire

BICS within two to five years of language learning whereas CALP can take from four to seven years. A lot of factors are involved in the acquisition of CALP, such as age, language proficiency level, literacy in the first language, etc.

Understanding the text features of different genres is an important strategy for ELL students. Successfully mastering characteristics such as the organizational structure (e.g., of a lab report or essay) are often essential to success within content-area classes. Helping ELL students to recognize these traits is a crucial academic support.

See also 1.2.

Skill 5.5   Selects and adapts appropriate materials for given instructional purposes to make content more accessible for English Language Learners

Content-based instruction (CBI) integrates L2 acquisition and the basic content areas of math, science, social studies, literature, etc. The most current research continues to find validity in the following:

- Learners do not learn L2 through singular instruction in the language's rules; they learn from meaningful interaction in the language.
- Learners will gain proficiency in a language only if they receive adequate input; i.e., language that is heard or read will start to make sense to a learner when they can build upon previous knowledge as well as understand context and cues.
- Although conversational fluency in L2 is a goal, speaking is not sufficient to develop the academic cognitive skills needed to learn the basic content areas.

When speaking, instructors should:
- speak slowly, but naturally, taking care to enunciate without raising the volume.
- use short sentences when explaining a concept or instructions.
- use instructional strategies like repeating or rephrasing.
- write new vocabulary, expressions, or idioms on the board for further reinforcement.

When solving word problems in math, the instructors should first:
- work through a word problem with the student step-by-step.
- demonstrate various strategies for problem-solving.

When providing contextualization, the instructor should:
- use facial expressions and gestures
- use realia (cultural objects).
- use visual cues, such as photos, drawings, videos, etc.
- use graphic organizers.

When giving directions, the instructor should:

- simplify complicated tasks by giving specific instructions such as, "Open to page 107. Read the story. Once you have finished, wait for the class to finish reading."
- periodically check for comprehension during the lesson.
- provide opportunities for learner interactions.
- Create cooperative learning groups, which are essential for English Language Learners with varying levels of proficiency; heterogeneous groupings help to improve academic performance, especially if ELLs have the opportunity to clarify concepts and ask questions in their primary language.

When checking for understanding, the instructor should:

- ask the learners to clarify the first, second, and continuing steps of a process.
- ask a "who," "what," "when," "where," or "whose" question.
- ask for clarification from the learner.

When correcting an error, the instructor should:

- NEVER embarrass or humiliate an English Language Learner.
- avoid corrections when possible and simply accept the ELL's efforts at language. Model the language correctly without comments.
- keep error correction to a minimum at first.
- emphasize that making mistakes and being corrected is a basic part of any learning process, especially when learning a language.
- focus on what a learner is trying to communicate rather than on how correct the communication is.
- restate the question or sentence correctly when the error interferes with understanding.

Included with the preceding strategies are the following reminders. Always announce and write down the objectives for a particular unit, use handwriting that is readable, develop consistency through daily routines, list step-by-step instructions, and use blended instructional approaches, whenever possible.

One of the great challenges of middle school and high school teachers is to make content accessible to students with limited proficiency in English. As subject-area content becomes more complex, ELL students may need even more support to make the content accessible. Teachers can offer tools like **graphic organizers**, infographics and charts to help support student comprehension of written materials or content from discussions. As students' language skills develop, they should be encouraged to employ these tools independently to support their own understanding. As noted in 3.5, these visual tools help ELLs visualize and organize information and promote active learning. Not only does the use of graphic organizers encourage creativity and high-order thinking skills, but it also helps students summarize and interpret texts.

In addition, (as noted in 3.7) ESOL teachers can:

- use or create materials that simplify the language of abstract concepts by retelling content information in easier English. Depending on the proficiency level of the students, teachers should use simple sentence structure and high frequency verbs.
- select materials that help students build connections and associations in order to access background knowledge or previously taught information. This can be accomplished through teacher-prepared outlines and study guides.
- present students with written as well as aural messages. Outline what you are saying on the chalkboard.
- allow students' use of native language for English language and concept development.
- model think-alouds to increase student comprehension. *Think-alouds* are oral demonstrations of the teacher's own cognitive processes or the strategies they use to comprehend a text. Students then try to incorporate these strategies to help themselves in the learning process. Teachers explicitly teach these strategies until the learners are able to use them independently.

Some English language learners (ELLs) know very little English but have a rich content background in their primary language. Other ELLs may have acquired intermediate or advanced English skills, but still have gaps in their content knowledge. In order for ELLs to become successful overall students, they need to learn both English and grade-level content. English language teachers support the teaching of **content area subjects** in the classroom, but at times they also need to teach them from the original text without the opportunity to simplify content for their students. These teachers can adopt certain strategies that will give additional support to ELLs in their learning of content-area subjects such as, math, science, literature, etc. Some of the strategies are as follows:

- *Introducing a text before reading*: Pre-reading activities may be designed to motivate student interest, activate prior knowledge, or pre-teach potentially difficult concepts and vocabulary. This is also a great opportunity to introduce comprehension components such as cause and effect, compare and contrast, personification, main idea, sequencing, and others. Some pre-reading activities could be showing a film on a related topic, conducting an experiment, going on a field trip, etc.

- *Cooperative learning strategies:* Cooperative learning is particularly beneficial for any student learning a second language. Cooperative learning activities promote peer interaction, which helps the development of language and the learning of concepts and content. It is important to assign ELLs to different teams so that they can benefit from English language role models. ELLs learn to express themselves with greater confidence when working in small teams. In addition to picking up vocabulary, ELLs benefit from observing how their peers learn and solve problems. There are a number of such group activities that help students gain content and language at the same time. An example is *team jigsaw* in which each student in a team is assigned one-fourth of a page to read from any text (for example, a social studies text), or one-fourth of a topic to investigate. Each student completes his or her assignment and then teaches the others or helps to put together a team product by contributing a piece of the puzzle. Another example is a literature circle for teaching literature.

- *Explicit teaching of reading comprehension skills:* English language learners (ELLs) often have problems mastering science, math, or social studies concepts because they cannot comprehend the textbooks for these subjects. Teaching comprehension strategies help students apply these skills to all subject areas. These skills include: summarizing, sequencing, inferring, comparing and contrasting, drawing conclusions, self-questioning, problem solving, relating background knowledge, and distinguishing between fact and opinion.

- *Multicultural literature* can be an effective tool to teach literacy skills in an English language classroom. It helps to acknowledge the diversity of cultures in the classroom, where students feel proud of their own culture as well as learn about other cultures. Multicultural literature not only celebrates different cultures but also helps students relate to the text at hand. Students are able to activate their background knowledge, thus improving their comprehension of challenging texts.

Skill 5.6   Applies knowledge of instructional strategies that help students build on their prior knowledge and experience

The introduction to a lesson is very important for three primary reasons. First, students need to be engaged. They need to know that the material they will be learning in the lesson is interesting and important. Intrinsically motivated students will work through challenges far more readily than those who are not.   Second, understanding what is expected (learning objectives and an idea of how topics relate) helps students know what they have to accomplish. It is far easier for a student to meet expectations when s/he knows what those expectations are. Third, students need to have their background knowledge activated. If they have ways with which to attach new knowledge to existing knowledge throughout the lesson, they will be more successful in retaining and utilizing the new knowledge.

Building vocabulary is an essential element of literacy development for ELL students. One method for teaching vocabulary and building prior knowledge about the content for readers is the language experience approach. According to Pressley (2008), good readers make use of background knowledge to make inferences that are necessary for understanding a text. This helps readers create new knowledge from the text (*top-down processing*). In light of this view, the language experience approach supports children's concept development and vocabulary growth while offering many opportunities for meaningful reading and writing activities. It also helps in the development of shared experiences that expand children's knowledge of the world around them. In this approach, students' attention is focused on an experience in their daily life such as taking a class walk to collect leaves, blowing bubbles, making popcorn, apple picking, or experimenting with magnets. Students are involved in planning, experiencing, responding to, and recording the experience. The teacher initiates a discussion eliciting narrative from the students while providing appropriate vocabulary. In the end, the students compose oral individual or group stories which the teacher writes down and reads with students.

(See also Skills 7.1 and 1.9)

Skill 5.7 **Employs various scaffolding methods (verbal, procedural, metacognitive, visual and instructional) to support learners' content-area learning**

Various types of cognitive scaffolding can help English Language Learners achieve success in various content-areas. Understanding how these methods work and which ones to use when, allows teachers to design instruction to maximize student language and content-area literacy and mastery.

Verbal scaffolding includes paraphrasing, prompts, think-alouds, synonyms and antonyms, use of wait time, teaching familiar phrases, songs, etc.

Procedural scaffolding relates to the way instruction is organized and includes: teaching, modeling, practicing and student application (essentially, presentation, practice and production). The way the lesson is organized builds towards student independence. It also relates to the grouping of students as activities may move from whole class, to small groups, to partners to independence.

Instructional scaffolding helps students understand what they are learning. Examples include: graphic organizers, templates and guides, compelling tasks, and resources.

Metacognitive scaffolding relates to students' thinking skills and provides students with opportunities and tasks to plan, monitor and evaluate their learning. Examples include: syllabi, schedules, learning goals and plans, draft assignments, practice tests, discussions, scoring guides and rubrics, self-evaluations, reflections on the class and on learning.

Visual scaffolding relates to the use of visual aids to help learners understand what they are learning. Examples include: images on smart boards or handouts, posters or images on the wall, videos to introduce concepts

If these scaffolding techniques are used to help students access language and content that is just beyond their comfort level, they will develop more independence, more content area knowledge, more subject-specific skills and more language proficiency.

Skill 5.8 Promotes the development of learning skills and strategies to support subject-area learning

All students face the challenges of learning new content in different subjects, but for ELL students, this challenge can be compounded by the additional need to learn new vocabulary and new language structures. Teaching specific learning skills and strategies can support ELL students in learning the language structures necessary to both understand and express learning in different disciplines while also helping them to master and integrate new content-area knowledge. For students with limited or interrupted formal school experiences, these can be essential tools.

Strategies to consider include:

- Note taking - Students need to learn to synthesize large chunks of information presented orally or in writing in order to remember and apply essential ideas. Note-taking strategies vary tremendously, and different students will respond better to different methods.
- Research - All students will need to do research in different subject areas. This is a challenging process that includes searching for information, selecting what is relevant, synthesizing it into usable 'chunks', and integrating it into writing or projects. Students need methods for finding, saving, and annotating. Some students will find this easiest with traditional paper and pen and a notebook while others will benefit from digital tools (like Evernote or Diigo) that allow them to save sources and then annotate them. Research is a cross-disciplinary skill that should be used in multiple classes, but the ESOL teacher will play a special role in supporting ELL students.
- Study skills - Students may need practice in how to review for a test or prepare for an assessment. Teachers can assist students in creating flashcards (digital or paper) or learning ways of review (quizzing oneself/a partner, reviewing notes, etc.).
- Test-taking - Particularly in an era of high stakes testing, students may need guidance on how to pace themselves during assessments, when to skip items for later review, how to create an outline, or simply following procedural directions.
- Building vocabulary - For ELL students in particular, content area vocabulary can pose a challenge. Students may need support in learning how to categorize words, how to use new terms in context, or even the importance of looking up unfamiliar words to determine meaning.
- Comprehension - Inference is an important part of reading comprehension. For students learning English, extra time is often needed to develop skills for recognizing implied meaning.

Skill 5.9 Creates learning opportunities that promote creativity, problem-solving, critical thinking and collaboration in real world contexts

Creating critical thinking and problem solving learning opportunities can help English Language Learners in several ways. They can learn to deconstruct texts and other information sources (written, digital, audio, visual, oral), they can learn to identify points of view and analyze evidence, and they can learn to apply critical and problem-solving skills to make better decisions for themselves and others. These skills promote English Language proficiency, content and subject-area knowledge and real world skills that students can benefit from on a daily basis.

Examples of ways to incorporate or include critical thinking and problem-solving opportunities include: debates, analyzing media and messages, considering and working through authentic problems in different subject areas. Combining these strategies with meaningful texts, real-world tasks and a positive classroom environment can help students develop key critical thinking and problem solving skills.

Providing students with opportunities to be creative can help them solve some of those problems as well as express their thinking and learning in meaningful ways. Creativity in the ESOL classroom can be fostered in some of the following ways: provide multiple ways for students to express their understanding and learning; provide graphic organizers that help students brainstorm and make mind-maps before researching; analyze and/or solve a problem; or create a text. In discussion or group work, give students time to think - don't be afraid of wait time. These strategies and others, when combined with meaningful texts, real world tasks and a positive classroom environment can help students develop their creativity.

Allowing and encouraging students to collaborate can help English Language Learners learn to work with others, to build strong speaking and listening skills, to understand multiple perspectives and to feel more connected to others. It is important that ESOL teachers structure these opportunities to collaborate very carefully, at least at first. Having clear goals and guidelines for the "what" and "how" of the collaboration, incorporating meaningful tasks and texts, providing lots of opportunity for students to reflect on the process and creating a positive classroom environment can help English Language Learners learn and benefit from the skills and habits of mind of true collaboration.

Creating structured opportunities with clear goals, methods and assessments for English Language Learners to develop their problem-solving, critical thinking, creativity and collaboration skills, habits and ways of thinking can enhance progress in literacy, knowledge and language production.

Skill 5.10   Demonstrates knowledge of appropriate assessment tools, adaptations, interventions and accommodations to assess English Language Learners' development in content-area, discipline-specific language and literacy

Some assessment accommodations for English Language Learners include:

- ELL students may have times extended on ELA and content-area assessments as well as on all Regents Examinations, if schools request the additional time.

The time extended can include the regular amount of time allotted for the test plus half of that time added on for English Language Learners.
- If schools wish to assess English Language Learners in small groups in a separate location or as individuals in a separate location, they may do so.
- English Language Learners in grades 3 - 8 can have proctors read listening passages three times on English Language Arts assessments and on the Regents Comprehensive Examination in English.
- In all State exams, with the exception of foreign language exams, ELLs may use bilingual dictionaries with one to one word translations.

For more information on accommodations, see NYSED's website on ELL and MLL assessment. (http://www.nysed.gov/bilingual-ed/schools/english-language-learnermultilingual-learner-assessment-testing-accommodations)

See also 3.9, 3.10.

COMPETENCY 6   ESOL PROFESSIONAL ENVIRONMENTS

Skill 6.1   Demonstrates knowledge of New York State regulations and standards relevant to programs for English Language Learners and English Language Learners with disabilities

Teachers should know, understand and follow New York State regulations as they work towards the achievement of state standards for English Language Learners and English Language Learners with disabilities. Regulations for English Language and Multilingual Learners can be found on the NYSED website. (http://www.nysed.gov/bilingual-ed/regulations/english-language-learnermultilingual-learner-regulations-compliance)

The state learning standards for ELLs can be found in New York State's Bilingual Common Core Initiative, launched in 2012. Information about these standards and about bilingual education in New York can be found on the EngageNY website (www.engageny.org).

As part of the guidelines set out by the State of New York, schools must provide academically rigorous instruction aligned to learning standards for all students. Services and accommodations should be provided for English language learners with disabilities that specifically address instructional needs. ELL support should be aligned with individual students' IEPs. Schools must also assess ELL students with disabilities with tools that take into account the combination of learning challenges and language proficiency.

In addition, schools must develop identification and exit criteria for ELL students with disabilities receiving services or participating in learning support programs. .

Skill 6.2   Demonstrates knowledge of historical and current court cases and government (state, federal) policies affecting ESOL instruction

In 1961, due to the large numbers of Cuban children who migrated to Florida, Dade County Public Schools became one of the first school districts to put a major bilingual education program into action. In 1968, the Bilingual Education Act, now known as Title VII of the Elementary and Secondary Education Act (ESEA), was passed by Congress, which provided funding for all school districts to implement programs for LEP students to "participate" in academic activities.

Through Title VI of the **Civil Rights Act of 1964** established that schools, as recipients of federal funds, cannot discriminate against ELLs: "No person in the United States shall, on the grounds of race, color, or national origin, be excluded from participation in, be denied the benefits of, or be subjected to discrimination under any program or activity receiving Federal financial assistance."

In 1970, this mandate was detailed more specifically for ELLs in the **May 25 Memorandum** "Where inability to speak and understand the English language excludes national origin-minority group children from effective participation in the educational program offered by a school district, the district must take affirmative steps to rectify the language deficiency in order to open its instructional program to these students." The memorandum specifically addressed the practice of placing ELLs, based on their English language skills, in classes with mentally retarded students; excluding them from college preparatory classes; and failing to notify parents of ELLs of school activities.

Since then, the Supreme Court ruled favorably in the following cases, which legally required school districts to improve educational opportunities for LEP students. **Lau v. Nichols** (1974): A 1969 class action suit filed on behalf of the Chinese community in San Francisco alleged that the school district denied "equal educational opportunity" to their children because the classes the children were required to attend were not taught in the Chinese native language. The Supreme Court ruled in favor of the plaintiffs, and determined a set of requirements that academic programs must provide.

Related to Lau v. Nichols, the Office of the Department of Health, Education and Welfare created a committee of experts, who established guidelines and procedures for local educational groups serving the LEP population. The "Lau Remedies" became guidelines for all states to assist in the academic needs of LEP students; the "Lau Remedies" also provided guidelines for "exiting" LEP programs.

Per Lau v. Nichols, the Supreme Court ruled that no student shall be denied "equal access" to any academic program, due to "limited English proficiency [se1]." In a later decision, **Castaneda v. Pickard** (filed in 1978 but not settled until 1981), a federal court established three specific criteria schools must use to determine the effectiveness of bilingual education programs:

- A program for English language learners must be based on pedagogically sound educational theory that is recognized by experts in the field.
- The program must be implemented effectively with resources provided for personnel, instructional materials, and space.
- The program must produce results that indicate the language barrier is being overcome.

The 1983 *A Nation at Risk* report, produced by the National Commission on Excellence in Education, concluded that the U. S. educational system was failing to meet the national need for a competitive workforce. This prompted a flurry of education reforms and initiated the National Assessment of Educational Progress (NAEP), which keeps an ongoing record of school performance. While general participation is voluntary, all schools that receive Title I money must participate. This includes low socioeconomic and minority students, which includes a large percentage of ELLs.

In December 2015, the Every Student Succeeds Act (ESSA) was signed into law, replacing No Child Left Behind. The ESSA is a reauthorization of the Elementary and

Secondary Education Act of 1965. The ESSA made some changes to the testing data required for ELL students.

Rather than requiring that all results for students learning English be included in a school's cumulative data, the ESSA allows schools to develop a plan for phasing in the inclusion of their results. Further, ESSA requires schools to report in great detail on the progress of ELL students. They must:

- Report on the number of ELLs meeting academic standards (even for four years after exiting any learning programs in place for ELL students);
- Determine their own policies and procedures for entering and exiting language programs;
- Assess English language learners within 30 days of enrollment; and
- In addition, English language proficiency must be a factor in determining school ratings.

Skill 6.3   Demonstrates an understanding of different settings/models of ESOL instruction and management strategies appropriate to each

Traits of effective models and types of programs for English Language Learners include high expectations from ESOL teachers committed to student success, engaging and challenging learning environments for ELL/ENLs, positive and dedicated school environments that include meaningful and effective professional development programs for all teachers and incorporate state and district standards, policies and regulations collaborative learning environments for students, parental involvement and authentic communication opportunities between all stakeholders.

There are different models and programs for English Language Learners. Below are some commonly used approaches.

ESL/ENL Programs
These include pull-out programs where English Language Learners spend part of each day receiving explicit English language instruction, resource centers where students from several different classrooms come together in an ESL/ENL centre to use resources and work on English language proficiency, and/or ENL/ESL class periods, where students take ENL/ESL as a class for credit (generally in middle school).

Bilingual Education Programs
Early-exit bilingual programs: Early-exit programs generally provide instruction in the ELL students' first language for only a short time. This instruction is phased out with the goal of moving students to the mainstream educational program quickly.

Late-exit bilingual programs: Even after English proficiency is determined, up to 40% of instruction continues to take place in the home language.
Two-way bilingual programs (or developmental bilingual programs): Language majority and language minority students are grouped together to learn English as well as the

minority language. Native English speaking students develop proficiency in a new language as ELLs develop English proficiency.

Additional programs for ELL/ENLs include Sheltered English programs that combine students of different language backgrounds together in classes for content-area learning. Instruction is in English with significant scaffolding to support students of different proficiency levels.

In Structured Immersion programs there is little or no ESL/ENL instruction. Teachers generally have strong skills in the students' home language and are able to support ELL students in their acquisition of English through content-area study.

Skill 6.4   Analyzes and applies issues and trends within ESOL evidence-based research and employs current resources to update and inform teaching practice

Most ESOL instructors know that what is considered good teaching practice has evolved over the years as understanding of language acquisition and attitudes towards bilingualism have changed. It is important to stay informed about current research-based teaching practice in order to provide the best possible learning opportunities for students. The term research-based refers to ideas and practices that have been systematically tested through experimentation or observation. Furthermore, the observed outcomes have been analyzed and often subjected to further testing with results published in peer-reviewed journals.

As new information emerges in the fields of linguistics and language teaching, successful ESOL teachers are able to adapt and improve their teaching practice. Professional journals like TESOL and TESL-EJ explore and explain issues and ideas in English language teaching. Results are published for additional review and provide teachers with insight into effective teaching methodology. In addition, online communities allow teachers to share information and ideas about innovative teaching practices that best support ELL students.

Skill 6.5   Demonstrates knowledge of and applies metacognitive strategies to instructional practice and professional behavior

Demonstrates knowledge of and applies metacognitive strategies to instructional practice and professional behavior

Effective ESOL instructors foster and develop metacognitive strategies in their students and apply these strategies to their teaching practice. This is sometimes called meta-teaching. One metacognitive strategy for teachers is to compare what is being taught with how it is being taught. When ESOL teachers reflect on how they are teaching, they can be more effective teachers. Part of being a metacognitive teacher is taking time to reflect on teaching experiences and making a conscious plan to improve elements of teaching practice - e.g., What is the best way for me to teach this particular standard/content or language skill to this particular group of learners at this particular time?

If a particular strategy isn't working, reflective teachers can look at how they are teaching in terms of presentation, groupings, assessments and activities and then make a plan to re-teach and/or teach again, incorporating what they have learned or noticed. Generally, this is most effective when a teacher selects a specific element of their teaching practice to improve.

Being a metacognitive ESOL teacher means being a more effective teacher because it entails making personalized and 'just in time' adaptations to teaching plans while teaching. Reflective teachers are better able to make decisions to improve student learning because they are more aware of the many decisions they make that affect instruction and learning.

Reflective educators who examine their impact on colleagues and students are more likely to hone their teaching practice and make progress towards meeting their own professional goals. This, in turn, has an impact on student progress and the overall professional environment in which English Language Learning takes place.

Skill 6.6 Sets goals and participates in professional development activities to refine teaching practice

After employing meta-teaching and metacognitive practices, ESOL teachers are better able to set goals for professional development to refine teaching practice. (See 6.5.)

Professional development activities, both formal and informal, are important ways to improve teaching practice. Conferences (online and in-person) offer opportunities to share resources and to find out about current research into effective ESOL pedagogy. Membership in professional organizations usually provides opportunities to find out about conferences and to receive regular updates about research.

Skill 6.7 Facilitates effective and timely communication between the school and families of English Language Learners to enhance language and learning achievement

Where possible, it is to the advantage of the ESOL instructor to be prepared to explain and if necessary suggest alternatives to the families of ELLs should educational challenges occur. Where parents are knowledgeable about their alternatives, they are better able to support their children and fully participate in the school community. Caring teachers know that external factors can affect student behavior and performance in school.

As advocates for students, teachers must also be alert to students' social and emotional well-being. Since these factors can affect learning and achievement, teachers must be prepared to communicate about these issues as well. Timely intervention can be the key to emotional and academic success.

See also 2.5. And 3.11.

Skill 6.8 Works within the school community to facilitate cooperation between stakeholders and acts as a resource by modelling and sharing effective teaching practices

ESOL teachers play an important role in creating an environment in which all stakeholders (students, families, teachers, and administrators) work together to support the learning of ELL students. Especially when communication is difficult because of language barriers, the commitment of the ELL teacher to bridging the gap can make a significant impact in bringing all stakeholders together to work towards supporting the academic, linguistic, and social/emotional development of the student.

By modelling effective teaching practices and sharing resources both with colleagues and families, the ESOL teacher can help to maximize the learning opportunities available to all students. Support to classroom or content-area specialists can be invaluable with helping them to foster a supportive learning environment and in establishing a strong relationship to their students with limited English proficiency.

Skill 6.9 Analyzes and applies the benefits of collaboration between the ESOL teacher, content-area teachers, colleagues and community members to provide enhanced learning opportunities for English Language Learners; modelling and sharing effective teaching practices

Analyzes and applies the benefits of (and facilitates) collaboration between the ESOL teacher, content-area teachers, colleagues and community members to provide enhanced learning opportunities for English Language Learners; models and shares effective teaching practices

When ESOL teachers model effective teaching practices and act as resources to other teachers, they are both supporting their students' language acquisition and also their integration into the mainstream classroom environment. Extensive cooperation between ESOL specialists and classroom teachers enables the sharing of information about student strengths and weaknesses. This facilitates opportunities for improving instruction as well as better communication with students and their families.

See 5.3 on collaboration, cooperation and partnership teaching.
See 2.5 on utilizing community resources.

Skill 6.10   **Acts as an advocate to ensure that English Language Learners and their families have full access to the resources of the learning community**

See 2.5

Skill 6.11   **Demonstrates knowledge of ways to advocate for, acknowledge and affirm cultural diversity in the ESOL classroom, the school, and the community**

For English language learners, embracing cultural diversity can be an essential aspect of creating a safe learning environment. Learning a new language while also learning subject-area content in that new language involves significant risk-taking. If cultural and linguistic diversity are seen as assets within the school and community, anxiety around language acquisition can be significantly reduced.

The ESOL teacher plays an important role in ensuring that cultural and linguistic diversity are embraced in the school instead of being seen as obstacles that must be overcome. If this can be achieved, ELL students are more likely to have a positive attitude towards learning and will therefore be more likely to succeed. Teachers may find many opportunities to ensure that cultural diversity is valued. Some situations to keep in mind include:

- Planning with colleagues;
- Faculty meetings;
- Curriculum reviews;
- School events; and
- Ordering of materials for class and school use.

See also 2.8.

COMPETENCY 7   ANALYSIS, SYNTHESIS AND APPLICATION

Skill 7.1   **Applies research based strategies and practices to personalize instruction to support English Language Learners' literacy, oracy and academic development**

The first step in personalizing instruction is for ESOL teachers to assess English Language Learners' proficiency in literacy and oracy. In addition, teachers might also take into account a learner's:

- age and grade level
- level of home language proficiency
- social-emotional well being
- comfort levels with group work and independent work
- proficiency and comfort level with the five core skills (reading, writing, listening, viewing and speaking)

After analyzing assessment data, teachers can make action plans for individuals and groups of students. Aspects of instruction that can be personalized include:

- Teaching tools and resources (including technology and media)
- Production tasks
- Revising communicative, academic literacy and content-based goals

An important part of any personalized action plan for students, particularly students who are not meeting language literacy or content-area goals, is for the ESOL teacher to communicate with families and with the students themselves about learning or performance gaps and about the strategies teachers are going to use to support ELLs development.

The WIDA English Language Development Standards cover some research-based essential actions strategies for effective instruction with ELLs. (https://www.wida.us/standards/eld.aspx#essentialactions)

A few are adapted below:

- Create and utilize language proficiency profiles for each student
- Design language teaching and learning with attention to the sociocultural context
- Create meaningful, language-rich, and safe environments for English Language Learners that provide them with differentiated language practice and use. This means providing ample time for students to practice who need more and appropriate challenges for students who need less. That way all students are working to their potential and no students 'finish' before others.
- Use instructional supports and scaffolds

- Communicate and plan with other teachers in order get to know students' strengths and challenges outside of your classroom. This can help in planning personalized learning opportunities inside it.

Finally, when students are encouraged to be metacognitive learners, their ability to take responsibility for and personalize their own learning increases. This results in students becoming more active learners and has a positive effect on English language and content-area learning.

Skill 7.2 **Applies an understanding of different settings/models of ESOL instruction and management strategies appropriate to each to discussions of the best ways to meet English Language Learners' needs**

See 3.1 and 6.3

Skill 7.3 **Utilizes data-driven assessment (both formative and summative) to identify student needs and to plan appropriate instruction**

Key questions when using data-driven assessment to plan instruction are:

Where is the data being stored?
Assessment data needs to be stored in a place and in a format that is easily accessible to ESOL teachers (and others involved in assessing the student, if required). In order to benefit from data-driven assessment, it is not enough to merely collect the data. It has to be used. In order to use it, teachers have to know where to find it and must be able to move efficiently between assessment data and instructional planning apps, programs, or notebooks.

What are the goals for the student?
With every assessment, whether formal or informal, there are proficiency, knowledge and/or skill goals for each student. It is essential that assessments allow students to demonstrate what they know, what they have learned, or what they can do. For this to happen, the goals of the assessment must be clear to the English Language Learners. It also helps to have individual student goals easily accessible when analyzing assessment data.

What standards/progressions are met/not met?
Several competencies and skills in this book describe the need for teachers to demonstrate knowledge of and understand state standards and progressions, including the Common Core and language proficiency standards. When using data-driven assessment to identify student needs and help guide instruction, ESOL teachers would benefit from having the standards and progressions easily accessible. This information can help teachers decide whether to re-teach a lesson or a part of a lesson with the whole class, with groups of students and/or with specific students who have not yet met the standards.

What is the plan?
Making a plan is essential in order to truly use assessment data to help English Language Learners. The plan should include actions that both ELL students and ESOL teachers need to take, as well as outlining the formative and/or summative assessments that will be used to measure progress.

When ESOL teachers use consistent formative assessment, it keeps them focused on student progress and gives them the opportunity to plan appropriate instruction that meets students' needs. It also keeps parents, administrators, counsellors and other colleagues informed as students develop their English language skills.

Skill 7.4 Analyzes assessment data to determine the language learning needs of students according to the New York Common Core Learning Standards

Here is a list of different Common Core standards to add to your lessons and help with student proficiency. Taken from the website:

For ELA: "The Common Core Learning Standards for English Language Arts and Literacy define general, cross-disciplinary literacy expectations that must be met for students (Standards) and characteristics of CCLS instruction. The Standards are organized into four overlapping strands: Reading, Writing, Language and Speaking/Listening. Because the CCLS present an integrated model of literacy, the Standards mutually inform one another."

ELA learning standards: https://www.engageny.org/resource/new-york-state-p-12-common-core-learning-standards-for-english-language-arts-and-literacy

Math Common Core concept: "Coherence in the curriculum means progressions that span grade levels to build students' understanding of ever more sophisticated mathematical concepts and applications. Rigor means a combination of fluency exercises, chains of reasoning, abstract activities, and contextual activities throughout the module."

Mathematics learning standards
https://www.engageny.org/resource/new-york-state-p-12-common-core-learning-standards-for-mathematics

See 7.3 for the importance of applying assessment to determine needs.

SAMPLE TEST

Competency 1.0: Language and Language Learning

1. **The study of morphemes may provide the student with**:

   A. The meaning of the root word.
   B. The meaning of the phonemes.
   C. Grammatical information.
   D. All of the above.

2. **Language learners seem to acquire syntax**:

   A. At the same rate in L1 and L2.
   B. Faster in L2 than L1.
   C. In the same order regardless of whether it is in L1 or L2.
   D. In different order for L1.

3. **When referring to discourse in the English language, which is the most important principle for successful oral communication?**

   A. Taking turns in conversation.
   B. Degree of intimacy.
   C. The setting or context of the conversation.
   D. Empty language.

4. **"Maria is a profesora" is an example of:**

   A. Dialect.
   B. Inter-language.
   C. Code-switching.
   D. Formulaic speech.

5. **Interlanguage is best described as:**

   A. A language characterized by overgeneralization.
   B. Bilingualism.
   C. A language learning strategy.
   D. A strategy characterized by poor grammar.

6. **"The teacher 'writted' on the whiteboard" is an example of:**

   A. Simplification.
   B. Fossilization.
   C. Inter-language.
   D. Overgeneralization.

7. **The creation of original utterances is proof that the L2 learner is:**

   A. Recalling previous patterns.
   B. Mimicking language chunks.
   C. Applying knowledge of L1 to L2.
   D. Using cognitive processes to acquire the L2.

8. **Which one of the following is not a factor in people changing their register?**

   A. Relationship between the speakers.
   B. Formality of the situation.
   C. Attitude towards the listeners and subject.
   D. Culture of the speakers.

9. **L1 and L2 learners follow approximately the same order in learning a language. Identify the correct sequence from the options below.**

   A. Silent period, experimental speech, private speech, lexical chunks, formulaic speech.
   B. Silent period, private speech, lexical chunks, formulaic speech, experimental speech.
   C. Private speech, lexical chunks, silent period, formulaic speech, experimental speech.
   D. Private speech, silent period, lexical chunks, formulaic speech, experimental speech.

10. **According to Krashen and Terrell's Input Hypothesis, language learners are able to understand:**

    A. Slightly more than they can produce.
    B. The same as they speak.
    C. Less than they speak.
    D. Lots more than they speak.

11. **Experts on bilingualism recommend:**

    A. The use of the native language (mother tongue) until schooling begins.
    B. Reading in L1 while speaking L2 in the home.
    C. Exposing the child to both languages as early as possible.
    D. Speak the language of the school as much as possible.

12. **The affective domain affects how students acquire a second language because:**

    A. Learning a second language may make the learner feel vulnerable.
    B. The attitude of peers and family is motivating.
    C. Motivation is a powerful personal factor.
    D. Facilitative anxiety determines our reaction to competition and is positive.

13. **Angela needs help in English. Her teacher suggested several things Angela can do to improve her learning strategies. One of the following is not a socioaffective learning strategy.**

    A. Read a funny book.
    B. Work cooperatively with her classmates.
    C. Ask the teacher to speak more slowly.
    D. Skim for information.

14. **How does the NYSDE determine an ELL's level of English language proficiency?**

    A. Administer the NYSITELL (New York State Identification Test for English Language Learners).
    B. Administer a home language questionnaire upon enrollment.
    C. A school representative interviews the student.
    D. Administer the TOEFL exam within the first 10 days of enrollment.

15. Activating prior knowledge or schema is particularly important for English Language Learners because:

A. It makes learning more meaningful for the students.
B. It aids in reading and listening comprehension.
C. It validates cultural knowledge.
D. All of the above.

16. Which of the following is not a cognitive strategy for second language acquisition?

A. Cooperating with others
B. Practicing
C. Analyzing and reasoning
D. Creating structure for input and output

17. Teaching decoding skills to ELL students of all ages is important because:

A. It makes reading more pleasurable.
B. It leads to greater fluency, which in turn leads to higher achievement in reading.
C. New York State mandates decoding skills for ELLs at all grade levels.
D. Fluency ensures a high level of reading comprehension.

18. Which of the following are potential benefits of the transferability of first/home language literacy?

A. Students can apply reading skills from their home/first language to their new/second language.
B. Teachers can use similarities and differences in the home language and the new language to teach learning strategies i.e. cognates.
C. Transferability builds on what students already know and makes second language learning easier.
D. All of the above.

Competency 2 – Knowledge of English Language Learners

19. Which of the following is NOT a characteristic of differentiated instruction?

A. Flexible groupings of students
B. Assessment of each student's needs
C. Self-paced learning
D. Varied ways of demonstrating learning and proficiency

20. One argument for instruction in students L1 is that:

A. Students with strong first language literacy skills are able to transfer those skills to learning English.
B. The parent community will appreciate that the school teaches other languages.
C. Being bilingual usually means better job opportunities.
D. All students should be treated as individuals.

21. New York State Commissioner Regulation Part 154 identifies various groups of ELL students. One of these groups is Students with Inconsistent/Interrupted Formal Education (SIFE). Which of the following is not a common characteristic of a student from this group:

A. May be unfamiliar with the routines of being in school
B. May not have strong literacy skills in her/his home/native language
C. May have gaps in content knowledge
D. May have anger management issues.

22. How can the reliability of tests to classify students be ensured?

A. Multiple raters of the student's result
B. Clear scoring criteria
C. Multiple assessment measures
D. All of the above

23. As an ESOL teacher, which of the following would be an important factor to consider in deciding whether a beginner English Language Learner has a learning disability?

A. Frequent mispronunciation of words
B. Difficulty using the correct gender pronouns
C. Below grade level literacy in his/her first language
D. Gaps in vocabulary

24. Select the answer that best completes the following statement.

_____ may affect a beginner female English Language Learner's participation in class.

A. Culture
B. Code-switching
C. Diversity
D. Metacognition

25. A teacher plans a very engaging activity in which students work individually to compete in solving a math problem. All students are actively participating. At one table, however, an English Language Learner clearly has the right answer but does not tell her peers. How could the teacher restructure the activity to encourage her to share her response?

A. Give prizes for the best answer
B. Have students work in groups
C. Correct the other students and tell them the girl got it right
D. Call on her and ask her why she didn't share her answer

26. Wait time is a particularly important consideration for teachers of English Language Learners because _____.

A. They may need more time to formulate how to express their answers.
B. They may have anxiety about speaking in front of their peers.
C. They may take more time to process the question from the teacher.
D. All of the above.

27. Literature that reflects the culture of English Language Learners is a potentially valuable resource because:

A. It is more interesting than regular literature for students.
B. By having a cultural context that makes sense, students can focus on comprehension.
C. By showing different backgrounds it promotes equality.
D. It will have familiar words in it for students whose first language is not English.

28. According to Schumann, acculturation of English Language Learners is not likely to be impacted by:

A. Whether they/their families plan on staying in the country for a long time
B. Whether they feel that the majority culture respects them
C. Whether their parents have good jobs
D. Whether they feel welcomed in the community

29. Social factors influence second language learning because:

A. Age determines how much one learns.
B. Gender roles are predetermined.
C. Perceived social status could affect the ELL's ability to perform well in the learning situation.
D. Many ELLS cannot ignore their social conditions.

30. Culture and cultural differences:

A. Must be addressed by the teacher in the ELL classroom by pointing out cultural similarities and differences.
B. Should be the starting point for learning about how culture affects the ELL's attitude towards education.
C. Positively affects how well ELLs perform in the language classroom.
D. May have strong emotional influence on the ELL learner.

31. A 5th grader has completed one year in the ESOL program but does not seem to make progress. Which of the following might indicate a learning disability?

A. Frequently code switches.
B. Needs extra time to answer questions.
C. Is able to decode successfully but has comprehension difficulties.
D. Dropping of the final consonants of words.

32. Anxiety and self-esteem are particularly big concerns for _____ English Language Learners.

A. Adolescent
B. Very young
C. New
D. All of the above

Competency 3 – ESOL Instructional Practices, Planning and Assessment

33. When the teacher is correcting a student's language, the teacher should:

A. Carefully correct all mistakes.
B. Consider the context of the error.
C. Confirm the error by repeating it.
D. Repeat the student's message, correcting it.

34. An ESOL teacher who encourages her students to keep track of their progress in English Language Learning is stimulating which learning strategy?

A. Metacognitive.
B. Affective.
C. Cognitive.
D. Social.

35. Content-based instruction suggests LEP students need an additional 5-7 years to master academic language. During this time period, content area teachers should not:

A. Correct the LEP's oral language mistakes.
B. Speak more slowly and enunciate.
C. Demonstrate new materials using various strategies to increase input.
D. Check frequently for comprehension by asking students to explain what was said to a classmate or back to the teacher.

36. The Schema Theory of Carrell & Eisterhold suggests that for learning to take place, teachers must:

A. Integrate content areas with ESOL techniques.
B. Emphasize all four language skills.
C. Present comprehensible input in a meaningful context.
D. Relate new materials to previous knowledge.

37. Identify one of the following methods of dealing with fossilization as not appropriate.

A. Ignore mistakes that do not interfere with meaning.
B. Work on items such as ending /s/ for third person singular in written work.
C. Teacher (or aide) corrects all errors in the papers.
D. Dictate correct sentences of patterns frequently used incorrectly by ELLs.

38. The most appropriate ESOL strategy for readers who do not read in their L1 is to:

A. Postpone reading until the ELLs acquire intermediate oral language proficiency.
B. Teach cognates and high frequency words.
C. Develop literacy in L1 first.
D. Use pull-out reading support in L2.

39. Which of the following is not an activity that Communicative Language Teaching (the Communicative Approach) should not involve?

A. Real communication - students, teachers and others interacting and communicating
B. Meaningful tasks - activities and tasks relate to real-world situations and matter to students
C. Instructor interact with students by way of commands and gestures with students responding physically
D. Meaningful language - language is applicable to contexts and situations the learner encounters or will encounter (social, academic, workplace, subject-specific, etc.)

40. The steps involved in data-driven instruction and inquiry are:

A. Assess, analyze, take action
B. Assess, analyze, reassess
C. Plan, instruct, assess
D. None of the above

41. Which of the following mandates the state requirements for learning standards for English Language Learners?

A. The No Child Left Behind Act
B. The Every Student Succeeds Act
C. Lau v. Nichols
D. The Common Core

42. Content, process and product are the primary areas that can be adapted to support English Language Learners through:

A. Parental Communication
B. Differentiation
C. Formative assessment
D. Transfer from L1 to L2

43. What is a crucial element of successfully integrating technology in the ESL/ENL classroom?

A. Developing effective management and instructional strategies
B. Ensuring all students have access to a device at all times (1:1 program)
C. Ensuring that all resources are available in the learner's first language
D. All of the above

44. Loughlin and Haynes (1999) suggest that ESOL teachers make content accessible by implementing which of the following practices?

A. Pre-teach vocabulary and concepts
B. Check for comprehension during instruction
C. Teach the material in multiple ways (e.g. using visual cues, hands-on activities)
D. All of the above

45. Teachers can employ _____ in order to provide authentic opportunities for student interaction and greater opportunities to perform productively in the target language.

A. Multicultural literature
B. Leveled readings
C. Flexible groupings
D. Scaffolding techniques

46. Formative assessment is an essential part of:

A. Deciding a student's reading level
B. Determining whether a student has a learning disability
C. Placing students in the appropriate learning environment
D. Determining student progress and planning instruction

47. A reliable assessment test for ELLs will have the following three attributes:

A. Validity, reliability, and practicality
B. Validity, reliability, and flexibility
C. Practicality, reliability, and privacy
D. Reliability, validity, and familiarity for students

Competency 4: Instructing English Language Learners in English Language Arts

48. What features of the New York State Bilingual Common Core Initiative- New Language Arts Progressions help ESOL teachers make ELA Common Core standards accessible to all learners?

    A. List of performance indicators
    B. List of linguistic demands
    C. List of key academic and grade level demands for each Common Core ELA standard.
    D. All of the above.

49. Incorporating prior knowledge into English language learning does not:

    A. Permit readers to learn and remember more.
    B. Cause poor readers.
    C. Help readers to evaluate new arguments.
    D. Improve comprehension.

50. Which of the following is not a benefit of an integrated approach to the five skills (reading, writing, listening, speaking and viewing)

    A. It is more engaging for students.
    B. It allows teachers to evaluate content and language standards.
    C. It facilitates better parental and family communication and interaction.
    D. It allows for more meaningful and authentic interaction between students.

51. Which of the following language theories about listening is no longer valid?

    A. Top-down listening processing relies on the listener's bank of prior knowledge and global expectations.
    B. Listening is considered a 'passive' skill,
    C. Bottom-up processing of listening refers to analysis of the language by the listener to find out the intended meaning of the message
    D. Verbal learning becomes easier when information can be chunked into meaningful patterns

52. The shift in the teaching of speaking skills has moved away from a focus on perfect accuracy towards a focus on fluency and communicative effectiveness. This has had an effect on the kinds of activities that ESOL instructors use to help English Language Learners develop their speaking skills. Which of the following approaches does not incorporate this shift?

    A. The Grammar Translation Method
    B. The Cognitive Academic Language Learning Approach (CALLA)
    C. The Natural Approach
    D. Total Physical Response

53. Which of the following is not considered a foundation literacy skill?

A. Understanding of print concepts
B. Ability to deconstruct complex literary and information texts
C. Phonological awareness
D. Word recognition

54. Choose the correct word to complete the sentence. ESOL teachers should _____ foundational English literacy skills for early stage language learners.

A. consider
B. disregard
C. prioritize
D. postpone

55. What is a valid conclusion that could be drawn from the claim that vocabulary development is crucial for reading comprehension?

A. It is difficult for readers to understand the content unless they know the meaning of most of the words in the text.
B. It is a good idea to have students memorize extensive word lists so that they understand academic, communicative and content-based vocabulary.
C. It is beneficial to have students take frequent spelling tests in order to master sight word vocabulary.
D. It is difficult for readers to make significant reading progress when they have poor reading comprehension skills.

56. Which of the following strategies can be used help English Language Learners understand complex texts of different genres?

A. Use an anchor text or experience before reading a more difficult text.
B. Set up a reading-buddy program with students from a younger grade.
C. Encourage parents to help their children with reading assigned for homework.
D. Voice and choice – let students read what they want to read

57. Freire's research asserts that the primary purpose of critical literacy is that:

A. Critical literacy provides a means for individuals to identify with the nature of social conditions and change them.
B. Critical literacy is an investigation into the motives and goals of an author or speaker.
C. Readers are critical consumers of information received.
D. Oppressed people obtain power through education and knowledge.

58. According to Peregoy and Boyle (and other researchers), what are the six traits of English Languages Learners' writing fluency?

   A. Fluency, organization, grammar, decoding, genre, sentence variety
   B. Fluency, organization, grammar, vocabulary, genre, sentence variety
   C. Organization, comprehending, creating, emerging, genre, sentence variety
   D. Organization, vocabulary, sentence variety, engagement, genre, style

59. Analyzing reading passages, reading model paragraphs and examples, outlining (planning and summarizing) are all techniques for helping students:

   A. Brainstorm good writing topics
   B. Address conventions of English grammar
   C. Produce text-based written responses and research based writing projects.
   D. Fulfill Common Core and grade level standards

60. It is important to include grammar-oriented activities because (choose two):

   I. It helps students understand how grammar contributes to meaning
   II. It helps students effectively communicate their ideas and to make meaning
   III. clear and precise
   IV. it helps students maintain past linguistic traditions so that language does not devolve into slang and colloquialisms
   V. it helps students make fewer spelling errors and careless mistakes

   A. I and II.
   B. I and III.
   C. II and III.
   D. IV and I

61. Which of the following is not an evidence-based vocabulary development method?

   A. Working with other teachers at grade level or subject area when designing important vocabulary lessons and/or reading about evidence-based approaches to vocabulary instruction;
   B. Ensuring that reading vocabulary lists emphasize important words and not just decoding;
   C. Working to create some word lists that are common to many subjects, and if not, making word lists available to subject-area teachers to help students practice;
   D. Read-aloud techniques: During this activity, students read their papers aloud, listen to errors, and correct them as they proceed.

62. The New Language and Home Language Arts Progressions are designed to help all teachers do all of the following, except:

A. Use differentiated linguistic and language scaffolds for students
B. Find specific lesson plans for content area demands
C. Create or select appropriate level formative assessments
D. Select specific language learning objectives

Competency 5: Instructing English Language Learners in the Content Areas

63. Tools like graphic organizers help English Language Learners to:

A. Help students to build vocabulary in the content area
B. Break down the content so that it is easier to process and plan for writing or projects.
C. Helps students practice their handwriting which builds literacy
D. Helps students assess progress they have made in the content area

64. All of the following statements are true except:

A. During collaborative activities, teachers and students actively work together.
B. Collaborative activities can also include interacting with people outside the classroom.
C. Collaborative activities must be oral and cannot be written.
D. Collaborative activities can take place in pairs, small groups, or large groups.

65. Purposeful discourse can be used to design learning activities across the curriculum. Which of the following is not one of the four major kinds of purposeful discourse?

A. Shared discourse in which language is used socially to communicate and share meaning in order to accomplish social goals (playing games or planning a short scene),
B. Fun discourse in which language is used for fun (singing songs and writing riddles),
C. Thought discourse in which language is used to imagine and create new ideas and experiences (writing poetry or critical thinking).
D. Practice discourse in which students practice tasks on which they will be assessed.

66. Nonverbal adaptations, elicitation adaptations, and questioning adaptations are examples of what kinds of modifications to help make language more comprehensible for students?

A. Modifications in student interaction
B. Modifications in teacher-talk
C. Modification in assessment tasks
D. Modifications in instructional materials

67. Collaboration between ESOL and content-area teachers is beneficial because by working together, teachers can:

A. Provide a greater level of consistency for students in terms of expectations
B. Ensure that students are showing consistent development across classes
C. Develop curriculum and instructional strategies that best meet the needs of all students
D. All of the above

68. Which of the following is not an essential element for effective collaboration?

A. The need to establish a clear conceptualization of the task
B. The incorporation of explicit goals for ESL development into curriculum and assessment planning processes,
C. The negotiation of a shared understanding of ESL and mainstream teachers' roles/responsibilities
D. The inclusion of a variety of similar activities in various content areas

69. Content and ESOL teachers should incorporate teaching academic skills in their lessons in order to help English Language Learners develop proficiency in language and content-area learning. Essential elements to include in teaching academic English include:

A. Integrate listening, speaking, reading, and writing skills in all lessons for all proficiencies.
B. Teachers slow down the rate of speech, pausing between major idea units
C. Teachers enunciate, careful to pronounce new words slowly so that students can understand
D. Teachers use a variety of techniques to call on students to ensure student involvement

70. When ESOL teachers understand the discourse features of various types of text, they can help English Language Learners to:

A. Improve reading comprehension in content-areas
B. Improve writing in content-areas
C. Improve vocabulary in content-areas
D. All of the above

71. The following ideas are part of which instructional theory/practice:

English Language Learners learn from meaningful interaction in the L2 language, and they will gain proficiency if they receive adequate input. Additionally, speaking is not sufficient to develop essential academic cognitive skills.

A. Content-based Instruction
B. The Natural Approach
C. TPR (Total Physical Response)
D. Sheltered Immersion

72. There are many recommended ways of adapting content in Content Based Instruction. Which of the following is not a category for adaptation in CBI?

A. Giving directions
B. Providing contextualization
C. Collaborating
D. Checking for understanding

73. When correcting an error, the instructor should never:

A. Embarrass or humiliate an English Language Learner.
B. Model the language correctly without comments.
C. Focus on how correct the communication is rather than on what a learner is trying to communicate
D. Restate the question or sentence correctly when the error interferes with understanding.

74. Fill in the blank. _____ can be used as a tool for English Language literacy in content-areas because it can help to acknowledge the diversity of cultures in the classroom, which improves student confidence and personal comfort levels, and help students activate their background knowledge, which improves their comprehension of challenging texts.

A. Technology
B. Visual Aids
C. Multicultural day(s)
D. Multicultural literature

75. Fill in the blank
The following are examples of types of _____.

Paraphrasing, prompts, graphic organizers, and guides, syllabus, schedules, learning goals, draft assignments, and practice tests.

A. Scaffolding
B. Adapting content
C. The natural approach
D. Collaborative activities

76. Which of the following is not an example of the way that explicit instruction of study skills and learning strategies supports subject-area learning?

A. It supports ELLs in learning the language structures necessary to understand and express learning in different disciplines
B. It helps students learn kinesthetically. Not all students are visual or auditory learners.
C. it helps English Language Learners to master and integrate new content-area knowledge.
D. It can really be useful for students with limited or interrupted formal school experiences because it gives them the tools to help themselves

77. Which of the following are examples of opportunities for students to be creative, solve problems, think critically and collaborate?

A. Debates
B. Analyzing media and messages
C. Working through authentic problems in different subject areas
D. All of the above

78. Which of the following accommodations may be allowed for ELLs during assessment?

A. Giving extra time.
B. Asking proctor to explain certain words or test items.
C. Paraphrasing the prompt.
D. Use of an English-heritage translating dictionary.

Competency 6: ESOL Professional Environments

79. Bilingualism of ELLs can be greatly improved by:

A. A block schedule.
B. Community's appreciation of the L2.
C. Speaking L2 in the school.
D. Interference occurring between L1 and L2.

80. Which of the following should be done prior to initiating a formal referral process for an ELL with possible learning disabilities?

A. A vision and hearing test.
B. A language diagnostic test.
C. Documentation of at least 1 intervention.
D. Consultation with principal about ELL's progress.

81. In the United States, in schools with large immigrant populations of diverse origin, the most commonly used model is with large immigrant populations of diverse origin, the most commonly used model is:

A. Submersion
B. Pull-out ESL/ENL
C. Specially Designed Academic Programs In English
D. Transition

82. Based on the ESSA (2015), schools are required to include ELLs in state-mandated testing:

   A. In mathematics and science after 2 years of enrollment.
   B. In English language arts and math after enrollment.
   C. In mathematics with 1 year of enrollment.
   D. In English Language Arts after 1 year enrollment (and excluded from counting math and/or ELA tests for the first year)

83. Which of the following instructional strategies would not be appropriate for ELLs with exceptionalities?

   A. Use of texts adapted to students disability.
   B. Practice testing opportunities
   C. Differentiated instruction.
   D. Lectures.

84. An ELL suspected of having learning difficulties:

   A. May present behavioral differences when asked to produce written work.
   B. Might demonstrate the ability to learn quickly.
   C. Should be analyzed for up to 10 weeks using ESOL techniques.
   D. May demonstrate the ability to solve problems not dependent on English.

85. Which of the following is a possible sign of the gifted ELL student?

   A. Normal development according to parental interview
   B. Speech delayed in L2
   C. Seems to solve logic problems with difficulty
   D. High academic performance in L1

86. Ways for teachers to act as an advocate for cultural and linguistic diversity include:

   A. Planning with colleagues and Faculty meetings
   B. Curriculum reviews; Ordering of materials for class and school use.
   C. School events
   D. All of the above

87. Metacognitive strategies in educators can help improve instructional practice and professionalism. Which of the following is an effective metacognitive strategy for teachers?

   A. Teachers read performance evaluations carefully
   B. Teachers read parent and student evaluations
   C. Teachers make detailed lesson plans several months in advance
   D. Teachers reflect on teaching making just in time adaptations

88. It is important for ESOL teachers to stay informed on issues, ideas and theories in language learning and the ESOL field so that they can:

A. Be better teachers
B. Be better colleagues and teacher models
C. Connect with others in the school and wider ESOL community
D. All of the above

89. What is the difference between Dual One-way and Dual Two-way Bilingual programs?

A. In Dual One-way programs students only learn one language
B. In Dual Two-way programs English Language Learners and native English Language speakers are in the same class learning two languages
C. Neither of these statements is true
D. Both of these statements is true

90. ELLs can earn a points towards bilingual seal of literacy for everything on this list except:

A. English Language Learners (ELLs) score 75 or above on two Regents exams other than English, without translation.
B. ELLs score at the Commanding level on two modalities on the New York State English as a Second Language Achievement Test (NYSESLAT).
C. ELLs present a culminating project, scholarly essay, or portfolio that meets the criteria for speaking, listening, reading, and writing established by the district's Seal of Biliteracy Committee
D. ELLs complete a detailed self-assessment on home language proficiency after meeting English Language proficiency criteria

ANSWER KEY

1. C	31. C	61. D
2. C	32. A	62. B
3. A	33. D	63. B
4. C	34. A	64. C
5. C	35. A	65. D
6. D	36. D	66. B
7. D	37. C	67. D
8. D	38. C	68. D
9. B	39. C	69. A
10. A	40. A	70. D
11. C	41. B	71. A
12. A	42. B	72. C
13. D	43. A	73. C
14. A	44. D	74. D
15. D	45. C	75. A
16. A	46. D	76. B
17. B	47. A	77. D
18. D	48. D	78. A
19. C	49. B	79. B
20. A	50. C	80. A
21. D	51. B	81. B
22. D	52. A	82. D
23. C	53. B	83. D
24. A	54. C	84. C
25. B	55. A	85. D
26. D	56. A	86. D
27. B	57. D	87. D
28. C	58. B	88. D
29. C	59. C	89. B
30. D	60. A	90. D

RATIONALES

Competency 1.0: Language and Language Learning

1. **The study of morphemes may provide the student with:**

   A. The meaning of the root word.
   B. The meaning of the phonemes.
   C. Grammatical information.
   D. All of the above.

The correct answer is C. Grammatical information.
The meaning of the root word comes from its source or origin, and the meaning of phonemes relates to sound. The correct answer is C, which gives grammatical information to the student.

2. **Language learners seem to acquire syntax:**

   A. At the same rate in L1 and L2.
   B. Faster in L2 than L1.
   C. In the same order regardless of whether it is in L1 or L2.
   D. In different order for L1.

The correct answer is C. In the same order regardless of whether it is in L1 or L2.
All language learners must progress through the same hierarchical steps in their language learning process. They go from the least to the most complicated stages, regardless of whether it is in the L1 or L2.

3. **When referring to discourse in the English language, which is the most important principle for successful oral communication?**

   A. Taking turns in conversation.
   B. Choice of topic.
   C. The setting or context of the conversation.
   D. Empty language.

The correct answer is A. Taking turns in conversation.
For discourse to be successful in any language, a set of ingrained social rules and discourse patterns must be followed. The choice of topic and the setting or contexts of the conversation are important elements of discourse in English, but not the most important ones. Empty language refers to discourse perfunctory speech that has little meaning but is important in social exchanges. In oral English discourse, taking turns is primordial. The correct option would be A.

4. "Maria is a profesora" is an example of:

A. Dialect.
B. Inter-language.
C. Code-switching.
D. Formulaic speech.

The correct answer is C. Code-switching.
Dialect is any form or variety of a spoken language peculiar to a region, community, social group, etc. Inter-language is the language spoken by ELLs that is between their L1 and L2. Formulaic speech refers to speech that is ritualistic in nature and perhaps used for social politeness rather than information.

Sociolinguistics is a very broad term used to understand the relationship between language and people, including the phenomenon of people switching languages during a conversation. One person may switch languages when a word is not known in the other language. Option C is the correct option.

5. Interlanguage is best described as:

A. A language characterized by overgeneralization.
B. Bilingualism.
C. A language learning strategy.
D. A strategy characterized by poor grammar.

The correct answer is C. A language learning strategy.
Interlanguage occurs when the second language learner lacks proficiency in L2 and tries to compensate for his or her lack of fluency in the new language. Three components are overgeneralization, simplification, and L1 interference or language transfer. Therefore, answer A is only one component of interlanguage making option C the correct answer.

6. "The teacher 'writted' on the whiteboard" is an example of:

A. Simplification.
B. Fossilization.
C. Inter-language.
D. Overgeneralization.

The correct answer is D. Overgeneralization.
In this case, the ELL has tried to apply the rule of /ed/ endings to an irregular verb to form the past tense verb, i.e., he has used "overgeneralization" to create an incorrect verb form. The correct answer is D.

7. **The creation of original utterances is proof that the L2 learner is:**

   A. Recalling previous patterns.
   B. Mimicking language chunks.
   C. Applying knowledge of L1 to L2.
   D. Using cognitive processes to acquire the L2.

The correct answer is D. Using cognitive processes to acquire the L2.
Recalling previous patterns, mimicking language chunks, and applying knowledge of L1 to L2 do not demonstrate organization and direction of second language acquisition. The ELL has not integrated the L2 into his or her thought processes. When the ELL is able to form rules, s/he is able to understand and create new utterances. Selection D is the correct option.

8. **Which one of the following is not a factor in people changing their register? The:**

   A. Relationship between the speakers.
   B. Formality of the situation.
   C. Attitude towards the listeners and subject.
   D. Culture of the speakers.

The correct answer is D. Culture of the speakers.
People change their register depending on the relationship between the speakers, the formality of the situation, and their attitudes towards the listeners and the subject. Answer D—culture of the speakers is not a reason for people to change their register.

9. **L1 and L2 learners follow approximately the same order in learning a language. Identify the correct sequence from the options below.**

   A. Silent period, experimental speech, private speech, lexical chunks, formulaic speech.
   B. Silent period, private speech, lexical chunks, formulaic speech, experimental speech.
   C. Private speech, lexical chunks, silent period, formulaic speech, experimental speech.
   D. Private speech, silent period, lexical chunks, formulaic speech, experimental speech.

The correct answer is B: Silent period, private speech, lexical chunks, formulaic speech, experimental speech.
The correct order is B.

10. According to Krashen and Terrell's Input Hypothesis, language learners are able to understand:

    A. Slightly more than they can produce.
    B. The same as they speak.
    C. Less than they speak.
    D. Lots more than they speak.

The correct answer is A. Slightly more than they can produce.
Krashen and Terrell's Input Hypothesis (*i* + 1) states that instruction should be at a level slightly above the language learner's production level. In this way the learner will have the basis with which to understand but will have to figure out the unknown language in context.

11. Experts on bilingualism recommend:

    A. The use of the native language (mother tongue) until schooling begins.
    B. Reading in L1 while speaking L2 in the home.
    C. Exposing the child to both languages as early as possible.
    D. Speaking the language of the school as much as possible.

The correct answer is C. Exposing the child to both languages as early as possible.
Research on bilingualism suggests that children should be exposed to both languages from birth where possible for maximum bilingual benefit.

12. The affective domain affects how students acquire a second language because:

    A. Learning a second language may make the learner feel vulnerable.
    B. The attitude of peers and family is motivating.
    C. Motivation is a powerful personal factor.
    D. Facilitative anxiety determines our reaction to competition and is positive.

The correct answer is A. Learning a second language may make the learner feel vulnerable.
The affective domain refers to the full range of human feelings and emotions that come into play during second language acquisition. Learning a second language may make the learner vulnerable because they have to leave their comfort zone behind. This discomfort can be especially difficult for adults who are used to being powerful or in control in their professions, but it also affects children and teens. Option A is the best selection here.

13. Angela needs help in English. Her teacher suggested several things Angela can do to improve her learning strategies. One of the following is <u>not</u> a socioaffective learning strategy.

    A. Read a funny book.
    B. Work cooperatively with her classmates.
    C. Ask the teacher to speak more slowly.
    D. Skim for information.

The correct answer is D. Skim for information.
Options A, B and C are all socioaffective learning strategies. Answer D is a cognitive strategy and the correct choice.

14. How does the NYSDE determine an ELL's level of English language proficiency?

    A. Administer the NYSITELL (New York State Identification Test for English Language Learners).
    B. Administer a home language questionnaire upon enrollment.
    C. A school representative interviews the student.
    D. Administer the TOEFL exam within the first 10 days of enrollment.

The correct answer is A. Administer the NYSITELL (New York State Identification Test for English Language Learners).
Although a questionnaire is given and an interview conducted before the NYSITELL, it is the results of the NYSITELL that determine an English Language Learner's proficiency level and program placement. The TOEFL exam is given to non-native (English) speakers wishing to enroll in university.

15. Activating prior knowledge or schema is particularly important for English Language Learners because:

    A. It makes learning more meaningful for the students.
    B. It aids in reading and listening comprehension.
    C. It validates cultural knowledge.
    D. All of the above.

The correct answer is D. All of the above.
Activating prior knowledge (schema) connects to students' previous experiences and potentially cultural background(s). Therefore, it can make learning more meaningful while also valuing the students' culture. Additionally, the context provided by prior knowledge aids in comprehension.

16. Which of the following is not a cognitive strategy for second language acquisition?

    A. Cooperating with others
    B. Practicing
    C. Analyzing and reasoning
    D. Creating structure for input and output

The correct answer is A. Cooperating with others
Practicing, analyzing and reasoning, and creating input and output structures are all part of the four basic cognitive strategies (plus receiving and sending messages, with the four together having the acronym, PRAC). Cooperating with others is a social strategy in the Socioaffective domain.

17. Teaching decoding skills to ELL students of all ages is important because:

    A. It makes reading more pleasurable.
    B. It leads to greater fluency, which in turn leads to higher achievement in reading.
    C. New York State mandates decoding skills for ELLs at all grade levels.
    D. Fluency ensures a high level of reading comprehension.

The correct answer is B. It leads to greater fluency, which in turn leads to higher achievement in reading.
When English Language Learners, regardless of age learn and practice decoding strategies, they will build automaticity, which leads to greater fluency in reading. Greater reading fluency, increases reading achievement. A, may be true but it is not a reason to teach decoding skills. C is false. New York State does not mandate the explicit teaching of decoding skills, although ESOL teachers are encouraged to do so. D is incorrect because without focused instruction in reading comprehension, fluency will only take a student so far.

18. Which of the following are potential benefits of the transferability of first/home language literacy?

    A. Students can apply reading skills from their home/first language to their new/second language.
    B. Teachers can use similarities and differences in the home language and the new language to teach learning strategies i.e. cognates.
    C. Transferability builds on what students already know and makes second language learning easier.
    D. All of the above.

The correct answer is D. All of the above
Even when the new language does not have the same alphabet, students with literacy skills in their first/home language will be apply those skills when acquiring literacy in their new/second language. For example, they will likely be familiar with the process for decoding. Many languages share common traits such as word order (like English with subject-verb-object) or cognates in vocabulary. Students who can transfer reading skills will find learning English easier.

Competency 2 – Knowledge of English Language Learners

19. Which of the following is <u>NOT</u> a characteristic of differentiated instruction?

    A. Flexible groupings of students
    B. Assessment of each student's needs
    C. Self-paced learning
    D. Varied ways of demonstrating learning and proficiency

The correct answer is C. Self-paced learning
Self-paced learning is not a feature of differentiated instruction. In an individualized program students may choose their own pace for learning or even what they learn, but differentiation as an instructional model does not do this.

20. One argument for instruction in students L1 is that:

    A. Students with strong first language literacy skills are able to transfer those skills to learning English.
    B. The parent community will appreciate that the school teaches other languages.
    C. Being bilingual usually means better job opportunities.
    D. All students should be treated as individuals.

The correct answer is A. Students with strong first language literacy skills are able to transfer those skills to learning English.
Research has shown that ELL students with strong reading and writing skills in their home or native language are able to apply those skills to learning English and to learning subject-area content in English.

21. New York State Commissioner Regulation Part 154 identifies various groups of ELL students. One of these groups is Students with Inconsistent/Interrupted Formal Education (SIFE). Which of the following is not a common characteristic of a student from this group:

    A. May be unfamiliar with the routines of being in school
    B. May not have strong literacy skills in her/his home/native language
    C. May have gaps in content knowledge
    D. May have anger management issues.

The correct answer is D. May have anger management issues.
Students with Inconsistent/Interrupted Formal Education may not have gone to school at all or may have missed significant amounts of formal schooling. This is particularly difficult for older students who may have significant gaps in skills and/or content knowledge and may not be accustomed to many of the school routines most students take for granted. The ESOL teacher may have to advocate on behalf of SIFE students to ensure that their issues are not viewed as learning disabilities.

22. How can the reliability of tests to classify students be ensured?

    A. Multiple raters of the student's result
    B. Clear scoring criteria
    C. Multiple assessment measures
    D. All of the above

The correct answer is D. All of the above.
Though it is not necessary for ALL of these factors to be in place to ensure reliable tests, these are all important ways that the ESOL teacher can help ensure that ELL students are properly assessed for placement in special services.

23. As an ESOL teacher, which of the following would be an important factor to consider in deciding whether a beginner English Language Learner has a learning disability?

    A. Frequent mispronunciation of words
    B. Difficulty using the correct gender pronouns
    C. Below grade level literacy in his/her first language
    D. Gaps in vocabulary

The correct answer is C. Below grade level literacy in his/her first language.
Though this could be related more to prior educational experience (or interruptions in that experience), below grade level literacy skills in the student's first language is the only item from this list that is a potential sign of a disability. The other three are common among all early stage language learners.

24. Select the answer that best completes the following statement:
_____ may affect a beginner female English Language Learner's participation in class.

    A. Culture
    B. Code-switching
    C. Diversity
    D. Metacognition

The correct answer is A. Culture.
If a student is from a cultural group that reinforces the idea that girls should be quiet and obedient, the student may be reluctant to participate in class, particularly if she is new English Language Learner. A teacher can work to change this by, for example, using wait time, creating situations in which all students are expected to speak, and/or developing a routine of calling on male and female students equally.

25. A teacher plans a very engaging activity in which students work individually to compete in solving a math problem. All students are actively participating. At one table, however, an English Language Learner clearly has the right answer but does not tell her peers. How could the teacher restructure the activity to encourage her to share her response?

   A. Give prizes for the best answer
   B. Have students work in groups
   C. Correct the other students and tell them the girl got it right
   D. Call on her and ask her why she didn't share her answer

The correct answer is B. Have students work in groups.
Some activities that seem very engaging may not 'work' with some students, especially new English Language Learners. They may be from cultural backgrounds that value cooperation over individual achievement. In addition, the student may not want to stand out because of anxiety over language proficiency.

26. Wait time is a particularly important consideration for teachers of English Language Learners because _____.

   A. They may need more time to formulate how to express their answers.
   B. They may have anxiety about speaking in front of their peers.
   C. They may take more time to process the question from the teacher.
   D. All of the above.

The correct answer is D. All of the above.
English Language Learners may experience all these factors when the teacher asks questions in class. This is another reason that teachers can/should consider alternative ways to let students answer some questions (on slips of paper, backchannel chats, at the end of class, etc.).

27. Literature that reflects the culture of English Language Learners is a potentially valuable resource because:

A. It is more interesting than regular literature for students.
B. By having a cultural context that makes sense, students can focus on comprehension.
C. By showing different backgrounds it promotes equality.
D. It will have familiar words in it for students whose first language is not English.

The correct answer is B. By having a cultural context that makes sense, students can focus on comprehension.
When a cultural context makes sense to them, students can focus on comprehension. Students who are still building English language proficiency may still struggle with books that deal with unfamiliar contexts. Even though they may understand the vocabulary in a book, meaning may be obscured by unfamiliar references. Even though it is entirely in English, a book that deals with a cultural experience that is familiar may allow students to concentrate on building vocabulary and comprehension skills. There is nothing about multicultural literature that is inherently 'more interesting' or 'equal'.

28. According to Schumann, acculturation of English Language Learners is not likely to be impacted by:

A. Whether they/their families plan on staying in the country for a long time
B. Whether they feel that the majority culture respects them
C. Whether their parents have good jobs
D. Whether they feel welcomed in the community

The correct answer is C. Whether their parents have good jobs.
Economic status is not generally viewed as a factor in acculturation. Instead it is the attitudes of the community that have a large impact on acculturation.

29. Social factors influence second language learning because:

A. Age determines how much one learns.
B. Gender roles are predetermined.
C. Perceived social status could affect the ELL's ability to perform well in the learning situation.
D. Many ELLS cannot ignore their social conditions.

The correct answer is C. Perceived social status could affect the ELL's ability to perform well in the learning situation.
If a student feels judged or looked down upon for his/her identity or language proficiency, this can have a negative effect on learning.

30. Culture and cultural differences:

   A. Must be addressed by the teacher in the ELL classroom by pointing out cultural similarities and differences.
   B. Should be the starting point for learning about how culture affects the ELL's attitude towards education.
   C. Positively affects how well ELLs perform in the language classroom.
   D. May have strong emotional influence on the ELL learner.

The correct answer is D. May have strong emotional influence on the ELL learner.
The skillful ESOL teacher may address culture and cultural differences, but frequently teachers are unaware of all the cultures and cultural differences they are dealing with. At the same time, it may be possible to determine how his or her culture affects the ELL's attitude towards education; however, it may well be something the young child cannot express or the adult hides for various reasons. Culture and cultural differences do not always play a positive role in the learning process. Culture and cultural differences may have a strong emotional influence on the ELL learner, whether it be negative or positive. Thus, D is our best option.

31. A 5th grader has completed one year in the ESOL program but does not seem to make progress. Which of the following might indicate a learning disability?

   A. Frequently code switches.
   B. Needs extra time to answer questions.
   C. Is able to decode successfully but has comprehension difficulties.
   D. Dropping of the final consonants of words.

The correct answer is C. Is able to decode successfully but has comprehension difficulties.
Answers A and B are normal ELL reactions to the stress of learning a new language. Answer D refers to a pronunciation error, which may be normal in the ELL's first language. Only C goes beyond the normal problems of ESOL and possibly into the realm of learning difficulties.

32. Anxiety and self-esteem are particularly big concerns for _____ English Language Learners.

    A. Adolescent
    B. Very young
    C. New
    D. All of the above

The correct answer is A. Adolescent.
The social pressure and self-consciousness that often accompanies adolescence can negatively impact English language acquisition. Adolescents may be particularly worried about looking foolish in front of their peers when speaking English or standing out for being different.

Competency 3 – ESOL Instructional Practices, Planning and Assessment

33. When the teacher is correcting a student's language, the teacher should:

    A. Carefully correct all mistakes.
    B. Consider the context of the error.
    C. Confirm the error by repeating it.
    D. Repeat the student's message, correcting it.

The correct answer is D. Repeat the student's message, correcting it.
To carefully correct all mistakes a student makes would raise the affective filter and probably cause the student to hesitate before speaking. Considering the context of the error gives the teacher insight into the student's learning but isn't a method of correction. To confirm the error by repeating it would suggest to the student that his or her utterance was correct and is not good practice. The best option is D, which corrects the error in a way that shows the student the correct form without embarrassing him or her.

34. An ESOL teacher who encourages her students to keep track of their progress in English Language Learning is stimulating which learning strategy?

    A. Metacognitive.
    B. Affective.
    C. Cognitive.
    D. Social.

The correct answer is A. Metacognitive.
This ESOL teacher is instructing her ELLs in strategies that make them aware of their individual learning. By being aware of their learning strategies, ELLs can compare their previous learning with their actual learning and measure their progress (or lack of).

35. Content-based instruction suggests LEP students need an additional 5-7 years to pick up academic language. During this time period, content area teachers should <u>not</u>:

A. Correct the LEP's oral language mistakes.
B. Speak more slowly, enunciate carefully.
C. Demonstrate new materials using various strategies to increase input.
D. Check frequently for comprehension by asking students to explain what was said to a classmate or back to the teacher.

The correct answer is A. Correct the LEP's oral language mistakes.
A far more effective method is to correct the LEP's mistakes when working on written work because there is a visual record of the mistake.

36. The Schema Theory of Carrell & Eisterhold suggests that for learning to take place, teachers must:

A. Integrate content areas with ESOL techniques.
B. Emphasize all four language skills.
C. Present comprehensible input in a meaningful context.
D. Relate new materials to previous knowledge.

The correct answer is D. Relate new materials to previous knowledge.
The schema theory of Carrell & Eisterhold suggests that schema must be related to previous knowledge or learning does not take place. When activated, schema is able to evaluate the new materials in light of previous knowledge. If the arguments made are convincing to the learner, he or she accepts them and integrates the new knowledge into his or her data bank. Otherwise, if the new materials are unconvincing, the new knowledge is rejected by the learner.

37. Identify one of the following methods of dealing with fossilization as <u>not</u> appropriate.

A. Ignore mistakes that do not interfere with meaning.
B. Work on items such as ending /s/ for third person singular in written work.
C. Teacher (or aide) corrects all errors in the papers.
D. Dictate correct sentences of patterns frequently used incorrectly by ELLs.

The correct answer is C. Teacher (or aide) correct all errors in the papers.
Peer correction is an effective way of dealing with fossilization. Both the ELL and his or her peer have the opportunity to analyze errors in a non-confrontational way.

38. The most appropriate ESOL strategy for readers who do not read in their L1 is to:

    A. Postpone reading until the ELLs acquire intermediate oral language proficiency.
    B. Teach cognates and high frequency words.
    C. Develop literacy in L1 first.
    D. Use pull-out reading support in L2.

The correct answer is C. Develop literacy in L1 first.
Once the ELL understands pre-reading strategies and how the written word is connected to the spoken word, the learner is ready to read. Once fluency is achieved in the first language, second language reading instruction can begin and be more successful.

39. Which of the following is not an activity that Communicative Language Teaching (the Communicative Approach) should not involve?

    A. Real communication - students, teachers and others interacting and communicating
    B. Meaningful tasks - activities and tasks relate to real-world situations and matter to students
    C. Instructor interact with students by way of commands and gestures with students responding physically
    D. Meaningful language - language is applicable to contexts and situations the learner encounters or will encounter (social, academic, workplace, subject-specific, etc.)

The correct answer is C. Instructor interact with students by way of commands and gestures with students responding physically.
This is a feature of TPR (Total Physical Response) a command-driven instructional technique.

40. The steps involved in data-driven instruction and inquiry are:

    A. Assess, analyze, take action
    B. Assess, analyze, reassess
    C. Plan, instruct, assess
    D. None of the above

The correct answer is A. Assess, analyze, take action.
Data-driven instruction and inquiry is an approach based on assessing and analyzing student data in order to adapt instructional plans to maximize student learning.

41. Which of the following mandates the state requirements for learning standards for English Language Learners?

   A. The No Child Left Behind Act
   B. The Every Student Succeeds Act
   C. Lau v. Nichols
   D. The Common Core

The correct answer is B. The Every Student Succeeds Act (ESSA).
The ESSA requires that all states have English language proficiency standards aligned with their academic standards. The No Child Left Behind Act was replaced with the ESSA in 2015. Lau v. Nichols was a court case, and the Common Core is a national set of standards that many states have adopted.

42. Content, process and product are the primary areas that can be adapted to support English Language Learners through:

   A. Parental Communication
   B. Differentiation
   C. Formative assessment
   D. Transfer from L1 to L2

The correct answer is B. Differentiation.
Differentiated instruction generally falls in three categories - content, process, and product. Teachers may differentiate in any/all of these areas in meeting the needs of students.

43. What is a crucial element of successfully integrating technology in the ESL/ENL classroom?

   A. Developing effective management and instructional strategies
   B. Ensuring all students have access to a device at all times (1:1 program)
   C. Ensuring that all resources are available in the learner's first language
   D. All of the above

The correct answer is A. Developing effective management and instructional strategies.
When technology use is planned carefully and managed effectively it can increase learning opportunities for ELL students. It is not necessary for all students to have a device; many schools make use of carts or labs in which access is shared. It is not reasonable to expect that all resources will be available in all languages.

44. Loughlin and Haynes (1999) suggest that ESOL teachers make content accessible by implementing which of the following practices?

A. Pre-teach vocabulary and concepts
B. Check for comprehension during instruction
C. Teach the material in multiple ways (e.g. using visual cues, hands-on activities)
D. All of the above

The correct answer is D. All of the above.
Teachers should demonstrate knowledge of techniques that create a positive learning environment for all students, which means that content needs to be accessible to students with different learning styles and language needs.

45. Teachers can employ _____ in order to provide authentic opportunities for student interaction and greater opportunities to perform productively in the target language.

A. Multicultural literature
B. Leveled readings
C. Flexible groupings
D. Scaffolding techniques

The correct answer is C. Flexible groupings.
Though all of these are valuable tools in working with ELL students, flexible groupings are used to provide opportunities for students to interact using the target language with their peers.

46. Formative assessment is an essential part of:

A. Deciding a student's reading level
B. Determining whether a student has a learning disability
C. Placing students in the appropriate learning environment
D. Determining student progress and planning instruction

The correct answer is D. Determining student progress and planning instruction.
For a, b, and c, more formal diagnostic assessments are needed for accuracy. Formative assessment is useful for seeing how students are progressing towards learning goals and designing instruction to help them meet them.

47. A reliable assessment test for ELLs will have the following three attributes:

A. Validity, reliability, and practicality
B. Validity, reliability, and flexibility
C. Practicality, reliability, and privacy
D. Reliability, validity, and familiarity for students

The correct answer is A. Validity, reliability, and practicality.
Valid assessments should measure what they assert to measure (not something else). Reliable assessments should yield similar results if taken a second time. Practical assessments are easy to administer, to assess, and test concepts and content similar to what students have encountered in class.

Competency 4: Instructing English Language Learners in English Language Arts

48. What features of the New York State Bilingual Common Core Initiative- New Language Arts Progressions help ESOL teachers make ELA Common Core standards accessible to all learners?

A. List of performance indicators
B. List of linguistic demands
C. List of key academic and grade level demands for each Common Core ELA standard.
D. All of the above.

The correct answer is D. All of the above.
Using the Teachers Guide to implement the Bilingual Common Core Progressions provides teachers with a valuable resource for implementing Common Core Standards in a Bilingual/ELL classroom. All of the standards (linguistic, academic and content) are in one place along with scaffolds to help ELLs achieve them in the four modalities.

49. Incorporating prior knowledge into English language learning does **not**:

A. Permit readers to learn and remember more.
B. Cause poor readers.
C. Help readers to evaluate new arguments.
D. Improve comprehension.

The correct answer is B. Cause poor readers.
Activating schema and incorporating previous knowledge into L2 learning will strengthen the learning process. It certainly does not cause poor readers.

50. Which of the following is not a benefit of an integrated approach to the five skills (reading, writing, listening, speaking and viewing)

   A. It is more engaging for students.
   B. It allows teachers to evaluate content and language standards.
   C. It facilitates better parental and family communication and interaction.
   D. It allows for more meaningful and authentic interaction between students.

The correct answer is C. It facilitates better parental and family communication and interaction.
Integrating the five skills does not really improve parental and family communication. This is more dependent on the ways in which the ESOL teacher communicates and supports classroom and home interaction.

51. Which of the following language theories about listening is no longer valid?

   A. Top-down listening processing relies on the listener's bank of prior knowledge and global expectations.
   B. Listening is considered a 'passive' skill,
   C. Bottom-up processing of listening refers to analysis of the language by the listener to find out the intended meaning of the message
   D. Verbal learning becomes easier when information can be chunked into meaningful patterns

The correct answer is B. Listening is considered a 'passive' skill.
Listening is not considered a passive skill anymore but a dynamic process, which makes a lot of demands on language learners.

52. The shift in the teaching of speaking skills has moved away from a focus on perfect accuracy towards a focus on fluency and communicative effectiveness. This has had an effect on the kinds of activities that ESOL instructors use to help English Language Learners develop their speaking skills. Which of the following approaches does not incorporate this shift?

   A. The Grammar Translation Method
   B. The Cognitive Academic Language Learning Approach (CALLA)
   C. The Natural Approach
   D. Total Physical Response

The correct answer is A. The Grammar Translation Method.
The Grammar Translation Method was one of the first formal methods of language teaching and involved students memorizing long lists of vocabulary words without any requirement to speak in the L2 language. The other methods all incorporate fluency and communicative competence.

53. Which of the following is not considered a foundation literacy skill?

A. Understanding of print concepts
B. Ability to deconstruct complex literary and information texts
C. Phonological awareness
D. Word recognition

The correct answer is B. Ability to deconstruct complex literary and information texts

The understanding of print concepts, phonological awareness, word recognition (and phonics and fluency) is all considered foundational literacy skills. B is a higher-level reading and analytical skill related to academic discourse, content-area knowledge and subject area skills.

54. Choose the correct word to complete the sentence. ESOL teachers should _____ foundational English literacy skills for early stage language learners.

A. consider
B. disregard
C. prioritize
D. postpone

The correct answer is C. prioritize

Prioritizing foundational literacy skills regardless of age, for early state language learners is essential, even though the temptation may be to focus on content learning for older students. Without mastery of these concepts, students will not fulfill their academic potential and high level literacy will remain a challenge. Considering teaching these skills is not enough – they must be a priority.

55. What is a valid conclusion that could be drawn from the claim that vocabulary development is crucial for reading comprehension?

A. It is difficult for readers to understand the content unless they know the meaning of most of the words in the text.
B. It is a good idea to have students memorize extensive word lists so that they understand academic, communicative and content-based vocabulary.
C. It is beneficial to have students take frequent spelling tests in order to master sight word vocabulary.
D. It is difficult for readers to make significant reading progress when they have poor reading comprehension skills.

The correct answer is A. It is difficult for readers to understand the content unless they know the meaning of most of the words in the text.
Vocabulary development is particularly important for beginner ELL students both to support comprehension and to avoid frustration. Even in more advanced literacy proficiencies, research shows that focused, meaningful and consistent vocabulary development helps English Language Learners build literacy, academic and content area skills. Answers B and C are both techniques that effective ESOL teachers do not use so much anymore, as long word lists are hard to remember in the long term and a focus on spelling can distract from vocabulary learning. Answer D is true but not really a natural conclusion from the question's claim.

56. Which of the following strategies can be used help English Language Learners understand complex texts of different genres?

A. Use an anchor text or experience before reading a more difficult text.
B. Set up a reading-buddy program with students from a younger grade.
C. Encourage parents to help their children with reading assigned for homework.
D. Voice and choice – let students read what they want to read

The correct answer is A. Use an anchor text or experience before reading a more difficult text.
Using an anchor text is a strategy suggested by Shanahan (2008) for teachers to help students to understand complex texts of different genres. Although a reading buddy program, Answer B, can help students feel more confident about reading, it won't necessarily help them understand complex texts (as they will be reading simpler texts). Voice and choice D, may help students engage with what they are reading but it won't necessarily help them understand complex texts, unless they choose complex texts to read.

57. Freire's research asserts that the primary purpose of critical literacy is that:

A. Critical literacy provides a means for an individual to identify with the nature of social conditions and change them.
B. Critical literacy is an investigation into the motives and goals of an author or speaker.
C. Readers are critical consumers of information received.
D. Oppressed people obtain power through education and knowledge.

The correct answer is D. Oppressed people obtain power through education and knowledge.

Various authors (Auerbach 1999; Brown, 1999; Hammond & Macken Horaik, 1999 and Hull, 2000) have stated that critical literacy provides individuals with a means to identify with and change social conditions. Lohrey (1998) spoke of critical literacy as an investigation into the motives and goals of an author. Van Duzer & Florez (2000) asserted that critical literacy goes beyond the basic literacy skills and asks readers to become critical consumers of information. Freire's assertion was that oppressed people obtain power through education and knowledge.

58. According to Peregoy and Boyle (and other researchers), what are the six traits of English Languages Learners' writing fluency?

A. Fluency, organization, grammar, decoding, genre, sentence variety
B. Fluency, organization, grammar, vocabulary, genre, sentence variety
C. Organization, comprehending, creating, emerging, genre, sentence variety
D. Organization, vocabulary, sentence variety, engagement, genre, style

The correct answer is B. Fluency, organization, grammar, vocabulary, genre, sentence variety

Decoding is a reading strategy and not really a writing strategy. Comprehending is a reading and listening skill and creating is more of a general process. Emerging describes a stage of proficiency and engagement describes learners' feelings about the learning task rather than a trait of writing fluency.

59. Analyzing reading passages, reading model paragraphs and examples, outlining (planning and summarizing) are all techniques for helping students:

A. Brainstorm good writing topics
B. Address conventions of English grammar
C. Produce text-based written responses and research based writing projects.
D. Fulfill Common Core and grade level standards

The correct answer is C. Produce text-based written responses and research based writing projects.
Analyzing reading passages, outlining and studying model texts are research-based practices that help students develop proficiency in producing text-based written responses and research based writing in content-area subjects.

60. It is important to include grammar-oriented activities in the ESOL classroom because (choose two):

I. It helps students understand how grammar contributes to meaning
II. It helps students effectively communicate their ideas and to make meaning
III. Clear and precise
IV. it helps students maintain past linguistic traditions so that language does not devolve into slang and colloquialisms
V. it helps students make fewer spelling errors and careless mistakes

A. I and II.
B. I and III.
C. II and III.
D. IV and I

The correct answer is A. I and II.
Grammar oriented activities can help English Language Learners connect language constructions to language meaning and help them communicate and understand their own ideas and others clearly. C and D are based on more traditional beliefs about the importance of teaching grammar and spelling and are not necessarily supported with evidence.

61. Which of the following is not an evidence-based vocabulary development method?

A. Working with other teachers at grade level or subject area when designing important vocabulary lessons and/or reading about evidence-based approaches to vocabulary instruction;
B. Ensuring that reading vocabulary lists emphasize important words and not just decoding;
C. Working to create some word lists that are common to many subjects, and if not, making word lists available to subject-area teachers to help students practice;
D. Read-aloud techniques: During this activity, students read their papers aloud, listen to errors, and correct them as they proceed.

The correct answer is D. Read-aloud techniques: During this activity, students read their papers aloud, listen to errors, and correct them as they proceed.
This technique is used to help students correct grammatical errors in their own writing rather than a strategy for fostering vocabulary development.

62. The New Language and Home Language Arts Progressions are designed to help all teachers do all of the following, except:

A. Use differentiated linguistic and language scaffolds for students
B. Find specific lesson plans for content area demands
C. Create or select appropriate level formative assessments
D. Select specific language learning objectives

The correct answer is B. Find specific lesson plans for content area demands
To find specific lesson plans, you would consult another resource. The Progressions help teachers match lesson plans to linguistic and content scaffolds, they help ESOL teachers design and select assessments to meet literacy objectives and they provide adaptations for applying the standards/progressions in specific grade levels.

Competency 5: Instructing English Language Learners in the Content Areas

63. Tools like graphic organizers help English Language Learners to:

   A. Help students to build vocabulary in the content area
   B. Break down the content so that it is easier to process and plan for writing or projects.
   C. Helps students practice their handwriting which builds literacy
   D. Helps students assess progress they have made in the content area

The correct answer is B. Break down the content so that it is easier to process and plan for writing or projects.
Students may include vocabulary terms when using graphic organizers, but their purpose is to help students focus on the essential information from content-area classes. Graphic organizers aren't used to measure progress over time although they may be used to assess content-area knowledge. There is no evidence that handwriting builds literacy.

64. All of the following statements are true except:

   A. During collaborative activities, teachers and students actively work together.
   B. Collaborative activities can also include interacting with people outside the classroom.
   C. Collaborative activities must be oral and cannot be written.
   D. Collaborative activities can take place in pairs, small groups, or large groups.

The correct answer is C. Collaborative activities must be oral and cannot be written.
Collaborative activities can be of just about any type - written, spoken, recorded, physical. Groupings are flexible and do not have to take place solely within the classroom environment.

65. Purposeful discourse can be used to design learning activities across the curriculum. Which of the following is not one of the four major kinds of purposeful discourse?

A. Shared discourse in which language is used socially to communicate and share meaning in order to accomplish social goals (playing games or planning a short scene),
B. Fun discourse in which language is used for fun (singing songs and writing riddles),
C. Thought discourse in which language is used to imagine and create new ideas and experiences (writing poetry or critical thinking).
D. Practice discourse in which students practice tasks on which they will be assessed.

The correct answer is D. Practice discourse in which students practice tasks on which they will be assessed.
If students are just practicing for a test, they are not participating in purposeful discourse. The missing discourse from this list is Fact discourse in which language is used to acquire new information and concepts.

66. Nonverbal adaptations, elicitation adaptations, and questioning adaptations are examples of what kinds of modifications to help make language more comprehensible for students?

A. Modifications in student interaction
B. Modifications in teacher-talk
C. Modification in assessment tasks
D. Modifications in instructional materials

The correct answer is B. Modifications in teacher-talk.
Enright (1991) put forward the above teacher talk modifications that could help make language accessible to the students. With a combination of these teacher-adaptations and learning activities, teachers can help English Language Learners increase foundational content, knowledge and skills.

67. Collaboration between ESOL and content-area teachers is beneficial because by working together, teachers can:

A. Provide a greater level of consistency for students in terms of expectations
B. Ensure that students are showing consistent development across classes
C. Develop curriculum and instructional strategies that best meet the needs of all students
D. All of the above

The correct answer is D. All of the above.
It is important, particularly when second language learners have multiple teachers, such as in middle or high school, that teachers communicate and collaborate as much as possible, for all of the above reasons. Where there is inconsistency, teachers should work to uncover what it is that is keeping the student from excelling in a particular class.

68. Which of the following is not an essential element for effective collaboration?

A. The need to establish a clear conceptualization of the task
B. The incorporation of explicit goals for ESL development into curriculum and assessment planning processes,
C. The negotiation of a shared understanding of ESL and mainstream teachers' roles/responsibilities
D. The inclusion of a variety of similar activities in various content areas

The correct answer is D. The inclusion of a variety of similar activities in various content areas.
Similar activities are not necessary in diverse subject areas for teachers to collaborate on language and learning goals. Without clearly conceptualized tasks, goals and teacher roles and responsibilities collaboration will be less effective and beneficial for integrating content and language area objectives for English Language Learners.

69. Content and ESOL teachers should incorporate teaching academic skills in their lessons in order to help English Language learners develop proficiency in language and content-area learning. Essential elements to include in teaching academic English include:

A. Integrate listening, speaking, reading, and writing skills in all lessons for all proficiencies.
B. Teachers slow down the rate of speech, pausing between major idea units
C. Teachers enunciate, careful to pronounce new words slowly so that students can understand
D. Teachers use a variety of techniques to call on students to ensure student involvement

The correct answer is A. Integrate listening, speaking, reading, and writing skills in all lessons for all proficiencies.
B, C, and D are additional techniques to adapt teacher talk to make content more accessible for students. A relates specifically to teaching academic skills in content-area and ESOL classes.

70. When ESOL teachers understand the discourse features of various types of text, they can help English Language Learners to:

A. Improve reading comprehension in content-areas
B. Improve writing in content-areas
C. Improve vocabulary in content-areas
D. All of the above

The correct answer is D. All of the above
When ESOL teachers understand discipline specific and interdisciplinary discourse features of different text types, they can provide students with contexts, scaffolds and background knowledge in reading, writing and vocabulary tasks in content-area classes.

71. The following ideas are part of which instructional theory/practice:
English Language Learners learn from meaningful interaction in the L2
language, and they will gain proficiency if they receive adequate input.
Additionally, speaking is not sufficient to develop essential academic
cognitive skills.

   A. Content-based Instruction
   B. The Natural Approach
   C. TPR (Total Physical Response)
   D. Sheltered Immersion

The correct answer is A. Content-based instruction.
Content-based instruction (CBI) integrates L2 acquisition and the basic content areas of
math, science, social studies, literature, and other subjects. The Natural approach
depends more on natural language acquisition in a classroom setting. TPR is based on
physical responses to teacher commands and not really related to content-based
learning. Sheltered immersion is a model for bilingual education programs and not an
instructional theory.

72. There are many recommended ways of adapting content in Content Based
Instruction. Which of the following is not a category for adaptation in CBI?

   A. Giving directions
   B. Providing contextualization
   C. Collaborating
   D. Checking for understanding

The correct answer is C. Collaborating
Skill 5.5 outlines specific CBI adaptations in the areas of giving directions, providing
contextualization and checking for understanding. Collaborating is a type of activity that
can help students engage in meaningful interaction it is not one of the key strategies for
making content more accessible. With CBI, ESOL and content-area teachers make
adaptations for students.

73. When correcting an error, the instructor should never:

A. Embarrass or humiliate an English Language Learner.
B. Model the language correctly without comments.
C. Focus on how correct the communication is rather than on what a learner is trying to communicate
D. Restate the question or sentence correctly when the error interferes with understanding.

The correct answer is C. Focus on how correct the communication is rather than on what a learner is trying to communicate
Focusing on how correct the communication is can intimidate students and create anxiety in students in both English language and content-areas learning. There is a time and a place for correcting errors that affect meaning or errors that are patterns and may become fossilized but the focus should always be on what the learners is trying to communicate.

74. Fill in the blank.
_____ **can be used as a tool for English Language literacy in content-areas because it can help to acknowledge the diversity of cultures in the classroom, which improves student confidence and personal comfort levels, and help students activate their background knowledge, which improves their comprehension of challenging texts.**

A. Technology
B. Visual Aids
C. Multicultural day(s)
D. Multicultural literature

The correct answer is D. Multicultural literature
Multicultural literature can be a very effective support in teaching literacy skills in an English language classroom, particularly when the content in the literature connects to the content or subject area.

75. Fill in the blank. The following are examples of types of _____.

Paraphrasing, prompts, graphic organizers, and guides, syllabus, schedules, learning goals, draft assignments, and practice tests.

A. Scaffolding
B. Adapting content
C. The natural approach
D. Collaborative activities

The correct answer is A. Scaffolding

The scaffolds are verbal, instructional and metacognitive scaffolds. They can help students access language and content that is just beyond their comfort level, which helps them develop more independence, more content area knowledge, more subject-specific skills and more language proficiency.

76. Which of the following is not an example of the way that explicit instruction of study skills and learning strategies supports subject-area learning?

A. It supports ELLs in learning the language structures necessary to understand and express learning in different disciplines
B. It helps students learn kinesthetically. Not all students are visual or auditory learners.
C. It helps English Language Learners to master and integrate new content-area knowledge.
D. It can really be useful for students with limited or interrupted formal school experiences because it gives them the tools to help themselves

The correct answer is B. It helps students learn kinesthetically. Not all students are visual or auditory learners.

Learning through hands-on or physical activities is not a factor in learning study skills and learning strategies. Even though students may incorporate innovative ways of studying into their personal learning strategies based on what they have learned, this would be a side benefit of study skill instruction rather than a clearly supported effect.

77. Which of the following are examples of opportunities for students to be creative, solve problems, think critically and collaborate?

    A. Debates
    B. Analyzing media and messages
    C. Working through authentic problems in different subject areas
    D. All of the above

The correct answer is D. All of the above.
Creating structured opportunities with clear goals, methods and assessments for English Language Learners to develop their problem-solving, critical thinking, creativity and collaboration skills, habits and ways of thinking can enhance progress in literacy, knowledge and language production.

78. Which of the following accommodations may be allowed for ELLs during assessment?

    A. Giving extra time.
    B. Asking proctor to explain certain words or test items.
    C. Paraphrasing the prompt.
    D. Use of general English-heritage translating dictionaries.

The correct answer is A. Giving extra time.
In New York State schools, ELL students may have times extended on ELA and content-area assessments as well as on all Regents Examinations. English Language Learners in grades 3 - 8 can have proctors repeat listening passages but they cannot paraphrase or explain certain words. ELLs may use bilingual dictionaries with one to one word translations but they may not use other translating dictionaries.

Competency 6: ESOL Professional Environments

79. Bilingualism of ELLs can be greatly improved by:

    A. A block schedule.
    B. Community appreciation of the L2.
    C. Speaking L2 in the school.
    D. Interference occurring between L1 and L2.

The correct answer is B. Community appreciation of the L2.
Motivation is always a key factor in language learning and when an ELL has community support for second language/cultural learning, bilingualism is greatly enhanced. Option B is the best option.

80. Which of the following should be done prior to initiating a formal referral process for an ELL with possible learning disabilities?

  A. A vision and hearing test.
  B. A language diagnostic test.
  C. Documentation of at least 1 intervention.
  D. Consultation with principal about ELL's progress.

The correct answer is A. A vision and hearing test.
Answer A is the correct selection since it eliminates the possibility of a childhood health issue before classifying a problem as a learning disorder.

81. In the United States, in schools with large immigrant populations of diverse origin, the most commonly used model is:

  A. Submersion
  B. Pull-out ESL/ENL
  C. Specially Designed Academic Programs In English
  D. Transition

The correct answer is B. Pull-out ESL/ENL.
SDAIE or Specially Designed Academic Programs in English is a structured immersion model that is not commonly used. The submersion model does not provide the necessary support that ELLs need and is in disfavor. Transition models provided approximately three years of BICS but frequently leave the LEP with almost no support while learning CALP. Today, the most commonly used model is B: Pull-out ESL.

82. Based on the ESSA (2015), schools are required to include ELLs in state-mandated testing:

  A. In mathematics and science after 2 years of enrollment.
  B. In English language arts and math after enrollment.
  C. In mathematics with 1 year of enrollment.
  D. In English Language Arts after 1 year enrollment (and excluded from counting math and/or ELA tests for the first year)

The correct answer is D. In English Language Arts after 1 year enrollment (and excluded from counting math and/or ELA tests for the first year)
Read the ESSA for additional requirements and exemptions for English Language Learners.

83. Which of the following instructional strategies would <u>not</u> be appropriate for ELLs with exceptionalities?

   A. Use of texts adapted to students disability.
   B. Practice testing opportunities.
   C. Differentiated instruction.
   D. Lectures.

The correct answer is D. Lectures.
Answer D is the correct one. Lectures are difficult for most people, and certainly for ELLs, whose attention span may be limited by their exceptionality and their L2 language proficiency level.

84. An ELL suspected of having learning difficulties:

   A. May present behavioral differences when asked to produce written work.
   B. Might demonstrate the ability to learn quickly.
   C. Should be analyzed for up to 10 weeks using ESOL techniques.
   D. May demonstrate the ability to solve problems not dependent on English.

The correct answer is C. Should be analyzed for up to 10 weeks using ESOL techniques.
Answers B and D indicate ability beyond the realm of language learning difficulties; they suggest gifted exceptionalities. Answer A suggests the ELL may be acting out to avoid producing work that is challenging or too difficult. The correct answer would be C, which indicates carefully documented follow-up to avoid placing an ELL in the incorrect environment.

85. Which of the following is a possible sign of the gifted ELL student?

   A. Normal development according to parental interview.
   B. Speech delayed in L2.
   C. Seems to solve logic problems with difficulty.
   D. High academic performance in L1.

The correct answer is D. High academic performance in L1.
Answer D suggests that excellent academic work in the first language would be the prime indicator of a student with exceptional abilities, especially if those abilities are apparent in the L2 also.

86. **Ways for teachers to act as an advocate for cultural and linguistic diversity include:**

A. Planning with colleagues and Faculty meetings
B. Curriculum reviews; Ordering of materials for class and school use.
C. School events
D. All of the above

The correct answer is D. All of the above

The ESOL teacher plays an important role in ensuring that cultural and linguistic diversity are embraced in the school instead of being seen as obstacles that must be overcome. If this can be achieved, ELL students are more likely to have a positive attitude towards learning and will therefore be more likely to succeed. Teachers may find many opportunities to ensure that cultural diversity is valued.

87. **Metacognitive strategies in educators can help improve instructional practice and professionalism. Which of the following is an effective metacognitive strategy for teachers?**

A. Teachers read performance evaluations carefully
B. Teachers read parent and student evaluations
C. Teachers make detailed lesson plans several months in advance
D. Teachers reflect on teaching making just in time adaptations

The correct answer is D. Teachers reflect on teaching making just in time adaptations

Although A and B may help teachers improve - they are more cognitive than metacognitive. By reading evaluations carefully, teachers are thinking about what someone else said about their teaching, rather than reflecting on what and how they are teaching. Making lesson plans far in advance does not involve reflection and, in fact, can make it difficult to adapt, if needed. Reflecting on teaching while it is happening is truly meta-teaching and allows for quicker lesson adaptation and effectiveness.

88. It is important for ESOL teachers to stay informed on issues, ideas and theories in language learning and the ESOL field so that they can:

   A. Be better teachers
   B. Be better colleagues and teacher models
   C. Connect with others in the school and wider ESOL community
   D. All of the above

The correct answer is D. All of the above.
It is important to stay informed about current research-based teaching practice in order to provide the best possible learning opportunities for students - acting as a teacher model, also helps make the school community more conducive English Language Learning and connecting with others, even outside the school, gives teachers a good cohort for learning new things, trying them out and talking about next steps.

89. What is the difference between Dual One-way and Dual Two-way Bilingual programs?

   A. In Dual One-way programs students only learn one language
   B. In Dual Two-way programs English Language Learners and native English Language speakers are in the same class learning two languages
   C. Neither of these statements is true
   D. Both of these statements is true

The correct answer is B. In Dual Two-way programs English Language Learners and native English Language speakers are in the same class learning two languages
In Dual Two-way programs English Language Learners and native English Language speakers are in the same class learning two languages. Dual One-way programs are made up of English Language Learners who speak the same language. New York State offers both options for English Language Learners (if there are sufficient numbers) in addition to a transitional bilingual education program which offers academic content in the home language.

90. ELLs can earn a points towards bilingual seal of literacy for everything on this list except:

A. English Language Learners (ELLs) score 75 or above on two Regents exams other than English, without translation.
B. ELLs score at the Commanding level on two modalities on the New York State English as a Second Language Achievement Test (NYSESLAT).
C. ELLs present a culminating project, scholarly essay, or portfolio that meets the criteria for speaking, listening, reading, and writing established by the district's Seal of Biliteracy Committee
D. ELLs complete a detailed self assessment on home language proficiency after meeting English Language proficiency criteria

The correct answer is D. ELLs complete a detailed self-assessment on home language proficiency after meeting English Language proficiency criteria
There are rigorous requirements for determining world language proficiency. See this website for more details: (http://www.nysed.gov/bilingual-ed/schools/new-york-state-seal-biliteracy-nyssb)

Interested in dual certification?

XAMonline offers over 19 NYSTCE study guides which are aligned and provide a comprehensive review of the core test content. Want certification success on your first exam? Trust XAMonline's study guides to help you succeed!

NYSTCE Series:

Communication and Quantitative Skills Test (CQST) 080
ISBN: 9781581978650

Assessment of Teaching Assistant Skills (ATAS) 095
ISBN: 9781581972603

Elementary Assessment of Teaching Skills- Written (ATS-W) 090
ISBN: 9781607873051

Secondary Assessment of Teaching Skills- Written (ATS-W) 091
ISBN: 9781607871552

English to Speakers of Other Languages (ESOL) 116
ISBN: 9781607874782

Library Media Specialist 074
ISBN: 9781581978636

Students with Disabilities 060
ISBN: 9781607874218

English Language Arts 003
ISBN: 9781607874799

Physical Education 076
ISBN: 9781581975796

French Sample Test 012
ISBN: 9781581978582

Biology 006
ISBN: 9781581972894

Chemistry 007
ISBN: 9781581978551

Earth Science 008
ISBN: 9781581976328

Literacy 065
ISBN: 9781607870579

Mathematics 004
ISBN: 9781581972962

Physics 009
ISBN: 9781581970425

Social Studies 005
ISBN: 9781581972658

Multi-Subject 002
ISBN: 9781607873587

Spanish 20
ISBN: 9781607870982

Don't see your test? Visit our website: www.xamonline.com